Night Thoughts

Compiled by SIMON WINDER

* * *

PENGUIN BOOKS

For CMJ

PENGUIN BOOKS

Published by the Penguin Group
Penguin Books Ltd, 27 Wrights Lane, London w8 5tz, England
Penguin Putnam Inc., 375 Hudson Street, New York, New York 10014, USA
Penguin Books Australia Ltd, Ringwood, Victoria, Australia
Penguin Books Canada Ltd, 10 Alcorn Avenue, Toronto, Ontario, Canada m4v 3b2
Penguin Books (NZ) Ltd, 182–190 Wairau Road, Auckland 10, New Zealand

Penguin Books Ltd, Registered Offices: Harmondsworth, Middlesex, England

This anthology first published 1998
1 3 5 7 9 10 8 6 4 2

Grateful acknowledgement is given to Papermac (Macmillan Publishers Ltd)
for permission to reproduce 'Channel Firing', 'The Darkling Thrush' and
'His Visitor' from *The Complete Poems* by Thomas Hardy.

Set in 10/12.5pt PostScript Adobe Minion
Typeset by Rowland Phototypesetting Ltd, Bury St Edmunds, Suffolk
Printed in England by Clays Ltd, St Ives plc

Contents

Publisher's Note

Night Thoughts is a selection of pieces, both poetry and prose, either written about the world after dark or – perhaps more evasively – giving the impression of having been written late at night. The aim of the anthology is to celebrate the extraordinary range of the Penguin Classics series and to point readers to remarkable authors they might not otherwise encounter. The sequence is entirely random – the chronology muddled and each author's works separated – in the hope of fostering such chance encounters.

At the core of the collection are the great 'night writers' of the seventeenth century with their dazzling ability to communicate human solitude, frailty and visionary religious hope: a sort of magical inwardness. These pieces find their musical equivalent in such chamber works as Dowland's *Lachrymae* or Purcell's *Fantazias* – pieces perhaps in reality written out-of-doors in bright sunlight, yet evoking an overwhelming atmosphere of late-night doubt. Perhaps the greatest example of all this genre (and one of the greatest masterpieces of English prose), the final chapter of Sir Thomas Browne's *Urne-Buriall*, is included here in its entirety.

'Night writing' has a fairly clear descent from Wyatt and Sidney through Shakespeare, Nashe and Donne to Browne, Herbert and Vaughan. The genre then declines: eighteenth-century literature seems almost relentlessly daylit – Young's *Night-Thoughts* are an enjoyable but strictly matinée performance and the tradition only really returns to the dark fully with Blake. From Coleridge through Arnold to Hardy the great 'night writing' continues, albeit rising from a quite different society. The illusion of the author as alone in the night and beyond human help which seems to emerge so effortlessly from Vaughan's meditations cannot work for the Victorians. Arnold's or Whitman's extraordinary poems show the poets battling with the strain of sustaining their nocturnal confidences while conveying them to a wide public: as though their respective silent starlit beaches are in reality thronged with cheerful and appreciative onlookers.

The collection ends with Thomas Hardy's 'Channel Firing', which unites many of *Night Thoughts'* preoccupations and, with its terrible intimations of the Great War, both ends the tradition and – rather less significantly – signals the chronological limit of Penguin Classics.

A wide variety of editorial spelling styles is used in the collection, from strict adherence to the original to a general smoothing out, reflecting different criteria used by academics in the course of Penguin Classics' lifetime. All textual notes have been dropped. A complete list of the books from which the works are drawn is given at the end.

Simon Winder

Night Thoughts

'Come, seeling night . . .'

MACBETH: Come, seeling night,
    Scarf up the tender eye of pitiful day,
    And with thy bloody and invisible hand
    Cancel and tear to pieces that great bond
    Which keeps me pale. Light thickens
    And the crow makes wing to the rooky wood;
    Good things of day begin to droop and drowse,
    Whiles night's black agents to their preys do rouse.

WILLIAM SHAKESPEARE,
from *Macbeth*, III, 2

To his Watch, when he could not sleep

Uncessant Minutes, whil'st you move you tell
    The time that tells our life, which though it run
    Never so fast or farr, your new begun
Short steps shall overtake; for though life well

May scape his own Account, it shall not yours,
        You are Death's Auditors, that both divide
    And summ what ere that life inspir'd endures
        Past a beginning, and through you we bide

The doom of Fate, whose unrecall'd Decree
    You date, bring, execute; making what's new,
Ill and good, old, for as we die in you,
    You die in Time, Time in Eternity.

EDWARD, LORD HERBERT OF CHERBURY

A nocturnall upon S. Lucies day, Being the shortest day

Tis the yeares midnight, and it is the dayes,
Lucies, who scarce seaven houres herself unmaskes,
   The Sunne is spent, and now his flasks
   Send forth light squibs, no constant rayes;
      The worlds whole sap is sunke:
The generall balme th'hydroptique earth hath drunk,
Whither, as to the beds-feet, life is shrunke,
Dead and enterr'd; yet all these seeme to laugh,
Compar'd with mee, who am their Epitaph.

Study me then, you who shall lovers bee
At the next world, that is, at the next Spring:
   For I am every dead thing,
   In whom love wrought new Alchimie.
      For his art did expresse
A quintessence even from nothingnesse,
From dull privations, and leane emptinesse
He ruin'd mee, and I am re-begot
Of absence, darknesse, death; things which are not.

All others, from all things, draw all that's good,
Life, soule, forme, spirit, whence they beeing have:
   I, by loves limbecke, am the grave
   Of all, that's nothing. Oft a flood
      Have wee two wept, and so
Drownd the whole world, us two; oft did we grow
To be two Chaosses, when we did show
Care to ought else; and often absences
Withdrew our soules, and made us carcasses.

But I am by her death, (which word wrongs her)
Of the first nothing, the Elixer grown;
   Were I a man, that I were one,
  I needs must know; I should preferre,
     If I were any beast,
Some ends, some means; Yea plants, yea stones detest,
And love; all, all some properties invest;
If I an ordinary nothing were,
As shadow, a light, and body must be here.

But I am None; nor will my Sunne renew.
You lovers, for whose sake, the lesser Sunne
   At this time to the Goat is runne
  To fetch new lust, and give it you,
     Enjoy your summer all;
Since shee enjoyes her long nights festivall,
Let mee prepare towards her, and let mee call
This houre her Vigill, and her eve, since this
Both the yeares, and the dayes deep midnight is.

JOHN DONNE

'Now for these wals of flesh'

Now for these wals of flesh, wherein the soule doth seeme
to be immured before the Resurrection, it is nothing but an
elementall composition, and a fabricke that must fall to ashes;
All flesh is grasse, is not onely metaphorically, but literally true,
for all those creatures we behold, are but the hearbs of the field,
digested into flesh in them, or more remotely carnified in our
selves. Nay further, we are what we all abhorre, *Antropophagi*
and Cannibals, devourers not onely of men, but of our selves;
and that not in an allegory, but a positive truth; for all this

masse of flesh which wee behold, came in at our mouths: this frame wee looke upon, hath beene upon our trenchers; In briefe, we have devoured our selves. I cannot beleeve the wisedome of *Pythagoras* did ever positively, and in a literall sense, affirme his *Metempsychosis,* or impossible transmigration of the soules of men into beasts: of all Metamorphoses or transmigrations, I beleeve onely one, that is of *Lots* wife, for that of *Nabuchodonosor* proceeded not so farre; In all others I conceive there is no further verity then is contained in their implicite sense and morality: I beleeve that the whole frame of a beaste doth perish, and is left in the same state after death, as before it was materialled unto life; that the soules of men know neither contrary nor corruption, that they subsist beyond the body, and outlive death by the privilege of their proper natures, and without a miracle; that the soules of the faithfull, as they leave earth, take possession of Heaven: that those apparitions, and ghosts of departed persons are not the wandring soules of men, but the unquiet walkes of Devils, prompting and suggesting us unto mischiefe, bloud, and villany, instilling, & stealing into our hearts, that the blessed spirits are not at rest in their graves, but wander solicitous of the affaires of the world; that those phantasmes appeare often, and doe frequent Cemiteries, charnall houses, and Churches, it is because those are the dormitories of the dead, where the Devill like an insolent Champion beholds with pride the spoyles and Trophies of his victory in *Adam.*

SIR THOMAS BROWNE,
from *Religio Medici*

My Midnight Meditation

Ill busi'd man! why should'st thou take such care
To lengthen out thy lifes short Kalendar?
When ev'ry spectacle thou lookst upon
Presents and acts thy execution.
    Each drooping season and each flower doth cry,
    Fool! as I fade and wither, thou must dy.

The beating of thy pulse (when thou art well)
Is just the tolling of thy Passing Bell:
Night is thy Hearse, whose sable Canopie
Covers alike deceased day and thee.
    And all those weeping dewes which nightly fall,
    Are but the tears shed for thy funerall.

HENRY KING

Summer on the Baltic

Nothing, in fact, can equal the beauty of the northern summer's evening and night; if night it may be called that only wants the glare of day, the full light, which frequently seems so impertinent; for I could write at midnight very well without a candle. I contemplated all nature at rest; the rocks, even grown darker in their appearance, looked as if they partook of the general repose, and reclined more heavily on their foundations. – What, I exclaimed, is this active principle which keeps me still awake? – Why fly my thoughts abroad when every thing around me appears at home? My child was sleeping with equal calmness – innocent and sweet as the closing flowers. – Some recollections, attached to the idea of home, mingled with reflections respecting the state of society I had been contemplating that evening, made a tear drop on the rosy cheek I had just kissed; and emotions that trembled on the brink of extacy and agony gave a poignancy to my sensations, which made me feel more alive than usual.

MARY WOLLSTONECRAFT,
from *A Short Residence in Sweden*

The Devil's Black Book

As touching the terrors of the night, they are as many as our sins. The night is the devil's Black Book, wherein he recordeth all our transgressions. Even as, when a condemned man is put into a dark dungeon, secluded from all comfort of light or company, he doth nothing but despairfully call to mind his graceless former life, and the brutish outrages and misdemeanours that have thrown him into that desolate horror; so when night in her rusty dungeon hath imprisoned our eye-sight, and that we are shut separately in our chambers from resort, the devil keepeth his audit in our sin-guilty consciences, no sense but surrenders to our memory a true bill of parcels of his detestable impieties. The table of our heart is turned to an index of iniquities, and all our thoughts are nothing but texts to condemn us.

The rest we take in our beds is such another kind of rest as the weary traveller taketh in the cool soft grass in summer, who thinking there to lie at ease and refresh his tired limbs, layeth his fainting head unawares on a loathsome nest of snakes.

THOMAS NASHE,
from *The Terrors of the Night or
A Discourse of Apparitions*

So We'll Go no more
A Roving

So, we'll go no more a roving
    So late into the night,
Though the heart be still as loving,
    And the moon be still as bright.

For the sword outwears its sheath,
    And the soul wears out the breast,
And the heart must pause to breathe,
    And love itself have rest.

Though the night was made for loving,
    And the day returns too soon,
Yet we'll go no more a roving
    By the light of the moon.

GEORGE GORDON, LORD BYRON

Mortification

How soon doth man decay!
When clothes are taken from a chest of sweets
    To swaddle infants, whose young breath
        Scarce knows the way;
    Those clouts are little winding sheets,
Which do consigne and send them unto death.

When boyes go first to bed,
They step into their voluntarie graves,
  Sleep bindes them fast; onely their breath
      Makes them not dead:
  Successive nights, like rolling waves,
Convey them quickly, who are bound for death.

  When youth is frank and free,
And calls for musick, while his veins do swell,
  All day exchanging mirth and breath
      In companie;
  That musick summons to the knell,
Which shall befriend him at the houre of death.

  When man grows staid and wise,
Getting a house and home, where he may move
  Within the circle of his breath,
      Schooling his eyes;
  That dumbe inclosure maketh love
Unto the coffin, that attends his death.

  When age grows low and weak,
Marking his grave, and thawing ev'ry yeare,
  Till all do melt, and drown his breath
      When he would speak;
  A chair or litter shows the biere,
Which shall convey him to the house of death.

Man, ere he is aware,
Hath put together a solemnitie,
And drest his herse, while he has breath
As yet to spare:
Yet Lord, instruct us so to die,
That all these dyings may be life in death.

GEORGE HERBERT

'What if this present were the world's last night?'

What if this present were the world's last night?
Mark in my heart, O soul, where thou dost dwell,
The picture of Christ crucified, and tell
Whether that countenance can thee affright,
Tears in his eyes quench the amazing light,
Blood fills his frowns, which from his pierced head fell,
And can that tongue adjudge thee unto hell,
Which prayed forgiveness for his foes' fierce spite?
No, no; but as in my idolatry
I said to all my profane mistresses,
Beauty, of pity, foulness only is
A sign of rigour: so I say to thee,
To wicked spirits are horrid shapes assigned,
This beauteous form assures a piteous mind.

JOHN DONNE

The City in the Sea

Lo! Death has rear'd himself a throne
In a strange city lying alone
Far down within the dim West,
Where the good and the bad and the worst and the best
Have gone to their eternal rest.

There shrines and palaces and towers
(Time-eaten towers that tremble not!)
Resemble nothing that is ours.
Around, by lifting winds forgot,
Resignedly beneath the sky
The melancholy waters lie.

No rays from the holy heaven come down
On the long night-time of that town;
But light from out of the lurid sea
Streams up the turrets silently –
Gleams up the pinnacles far and free –
Up domes – up spires – up kingly halls –
Up fanes – up Babylon-like walls –
Up shadowy long-forgotten bowers
Of sculptured ivy and stone flowers –
Up many and many a marvellous shrine
Whose wreathèd friezes intertwine
The viol, the violet, and the vine.
Resignedly beneath the sky
The melancholy waters lie.
So blend the turrets and shadows there
That all seem pendulous in air,
While from proud tower in the town
Death looks gigantically down.

There open fanes and gaping graves
Yawn level with the luminous waves;
But not the riches there that lie
In each idol's diamond eye –
Not the gaily-jewelled dead
Tempt the waters from their bed;
For no ripples curl, alas!
Along that wilderness of glass –
No swellings tell that winds may be
Upon some far-off happier sea –
No heavings hint that winds have been
On seas less hideously serene.

EDGAR ALLAN POE

'Now the hungry lion roars'

PUCK: Now the hungry lion roars
And the wolf behowls the moon,
Whilst the heavy ploughman snores
All with weary task foredone.
Now the wasted brands do glow
Whilst the screech-owl, screeching loud,
Puts the wretch that lies in woe
In remembrance of a shroud.
Now it is the time of night
That the graves, all gaping wide,
Every one lets forth his sprite
In the churchway paths to glide.
And we fairies, that do run
By the triple Hecate's team,
From the presence of the sun
Following darkness like a dream,

Now are frolic. Not a mouse
Shall disturb this hallowed house.
I am sent with broom before
To sweep the dust behind the door.

WILLIAM SHAKESPEARE,
from *A Midsummer Night's Dream*, V, 1

'Why did I laugh tonight?'

Why did I laugh tonight? No voice will tell:
  No God, no Demon of severe response,
Deigns to reply from Heaven or from Hell.
  Then to my human heart I turn at once –
Heart! thou and I are here sad and alone;
  Say, wherefore did I laugh! O mortal pain!
O Darkness! Darkness! ever must I moan,
  To question Heaven and Hell and Heart in vain.
Why did I laugh? I know this being's lease
  My fancy to its utmost blisses spreads;
Yet could I on this very midnight cease,
  And the world's gaudy ensigns see in shreds.
Verse, Fame, and Beauty are intense indeed,
  But Death intenser – Death is Life's high meed.

JOHN KEATS

'Th'en'my of life, decayer of all kind'

Th'en'my of life, decayer of all kind,
That with his cold withers away the green,
This other night me in my bed did find
And offered me to rid my fever clean,
And I did grant, so did despair me blind.
He drew his bow with arrow sharp and keen
And strake the place where love had hit before
And drave the first dart deeper more and more.

SIR THOMAS WYATT

The Glance

When first thy sweet and gracious eye
Vouchsafed ev'n in the midst of youth and night
To look upon me, who before did lie
              Welt'ring in sin;
    I felt a sug'red strange delight,
Passing all cordials made by any art,
Bedew, embalm, and overrun my heart,
              And take it in.

Since that time many a bitter storm
My soul hath felt, ev'n able to destroy,
Had the malicious and ill-meaning harm
              His swing and sway:
    But still thy sweet original joy
Sprung from thine eye, did work within my soul,
And surging griefs, when they grew bold, control,
              And got the day.

If thy first glance so powerful be,
A mirth but opened and sealed up again;
What wonders shall we feel, when we shall see
    Thy full-eyed love!
   When thou shalt look us out of pain,
And one aspect of thine spend in delight
More than a thousand suns disburse in light,
    In heav'n above.

GEORGE HERBERT

'Now winter nights enlarge'

Now winter nights enlarge
   The number of their houres,
And clouds their stormes discharge
   Upon the ayrie towres,
Let now the chimneys blaze,
   And cups o'erflow with wine:
Let well-tun'd words amaze
   With harmonie divine.
Now yellow waxen lights
   Shall waite on hunny Love,
While youthfull Revels, Masks, and Courtly sights,
   Sleepes leaden spels remove.

This time doth well dispence
   With lovers long discourse;
Much speech hath some defence,
   Though beauty no remorse.

All doe not all things well;
   Some measures comely tread;
Some knotted Ridles tell;
   Some Poems smoothly read.

The Summer hath his joyes,
   And Winter his delights;
Though Love and all his pleasures are but toyes,
   They shorten tedious nights.

THOMAS CAMPION

Of many Worlds in this World

Just like unto a *Nest of Boxes* round,
Degrees of *sizes* within each *Boxe* are found.
So in this *World*, may many *Worlds* more be,
Thinner, and lesse, and lesse still by degree;
Although they are not subject to our *Sense*,
A *World* may be no bigger than *two-pence*.
Nature is curious, and such *worke* may make,
That our dull *Sense* can never finde, but scape.
For *Creatures*, small as *Atomes*, may be there,
If every *Atome* a *Creatures Figure* beare.
If foure *Atomes* a *World* can make, then see,
What severall *Worlds* might in an *Eare-ring* bee.
For *Millions* of these *Atomes* may bee in
The *Head* of one *small*, little, *single Pin*.
And if thus *small*, then *Ladies* well may weare
A *World of Worlds*, as *Pendents* in each *Eare*.

MARGARET CAVENDISH,
Duchess of Newcastle

The Pains of Sleep

Ere on my bed my limbs I lay,
It hath not been my use to pray
With moving lips or bended knees;
But silently, by slow degrees,
My spirit I to Love compose,
In humble trust mine eye-lids close,
With reverential resignation,
No wish conceived, no thought exprest,
Only a sense of supplication;
A sense o'er all my soul imprest
That I am weak, yet not unblest,
Since in me, round me, every where
Eternal strength and wisdom are.

But yester-night I prayed aloud
In anguish and in agony,
Up-starting from the fiendish crowd
Of shapes and thoughts that tortured me:
A lurid light, a tramping throng,
Sense of intolerable wrong,
And whom I scorned, those only strong!

Thirst of revenge, the powerless will
Still baffled, and yet burning still!
Desire with loathing strangely mixed
On wild or hateful objects fixed.
Fantastic passions! maddening brawl!
And shame and terror over all!
Deeds to be hid which were not hid,
Which all confused I could not know,

Whether I suffered, or I did:
For all seemed guilt, remorse or woe,
My own or others still the same
Life-stifling fear, soul-stifling shame.

So two nights passed: the night's dismay
Saddened and stunned the coming day.
Sleep, the wide blessing, seemed to me
Distemper's worst calamity.
The third night, when my own loud scream
Had waked me from the fiendish dream,
O'ercome with sufferings strange and wild,
I wept as I had been a child;
And having thus by tears subdued
My anguish to a milder mood,
Such punishments, I said, were due
To natures deepliest stained with sin, –
For aye entempesting anew
The unfathomable hell within
The horror of their deeds to view,
To know and loathe, yet wish and do!
Such griefs with such men well agree,
But wherefore, wherefore fall on me?
To be believed is all I need,
And whom I love, I love indeed.

SAMUEL TAYLOR COLERIDGE

'I am naturally bashfull'

I am naturally bashfull, nor hath conversation, age, or travell, beene able to effront, or enharden me, yet I have one part of modesty, which I have seldome discovered in another, that is (to speake truly) I am not so much afraid of death, as ashamed thereof; tis the very disgrace and ignominy of our natures, that in a moment can so disfigure us that our nearest friends, Wife, and Children stand afraid and start at us. The Birds and Beasts of the field that before in a naturall feare obeyed us, forgetting all allegiance begin to prey upon us. This very conceite hath in a tempest disposed and left me willing to be swallowed up in the abysse of waters; wherein I had perished, unseene, unpityed, without wondring eyes, teares of pity, Lectures of mortality, and none had said, *quantum mutatus ab illo*! Not that I am ashamed of the Anatomy of my parts, or can accuse nature for playing the bungler in any part of me, or my owne vitious life for contracting any shamefull disease upon me, whereby I might not call my selfe as wholesome a morsell for the wormes as any.

SIR THOMAS BROWNE,
from *Religio Medici*

'How many thousand of my poorest subjects'

KING HENRY IV: How many thousand of my poorest subjects
  Are at this hour asleep! O sleep, O gentle sleep,
  Nature's soft nurse, how have I frighted thee,
  That thou no more wilt weigh my eyelids down
  And steep my senses in forgetfulness?
  Why rather, sleep, liest thou in smoky cribs,
  Upon uneasy pallets stretching thee,
  And hushed with buzzing night-flies to thy slumber,
  Than in the perfumed chambers of the great,
  Under the canopies of costly state,
  And lulled with sound of sweetest melody?
  O thou dull god, why liest thou with the vile
  In loathsome beds, and leavest the kingly couch
  A watch-case, or a common 'larum-bell?
  Wilt thou upon the high and giddy mast
  Seal up the ship-boy's eyes, and rock his brains
  In cradle of the rude imperious surge,
  And in the visitation of the winds,
  Who take the ruffian billows by the top,
  Curling their monstrous heads, and hanging them
  With deafing clamour in the slippery clouds,
  That with the hurly death itself awakes?
  Canst thou, O partial sleep, give thy repose
  To the wet sea-son in an hour so rude,
  And in the calmest and most stillest night,
  With all appliances and means to boot,
  Deny it to a king? Then happy low, lie down!
  Uneasy lies the head that wears a crown.

WILLIAM SHAKESPEARE,
from *Henry IV, Part Two, III, 1*

A Myriad Demons

What do we talk of one devil? There is not a room in any man's house but is pestered and close-packed with a camp-royal of devils. Chrisostom saith the air and earth are three parts inhabited with spirits. Hereunto the philosopher alluded when he said nature made no voidness in the whole universal; for no place (be it no bigger than a pock-hole in a man's face) but is close thronged with them. Infinite millions of them will hang swarming about a worm-eaten nose.

Don Lucifer himself, their grand Capitano, asketh no better throne than a blear eye to set up his state in. Upon a hair they will sit like a nit, and overdredge a bald pate like a white scurf. The wrinkles in old witches' visages they eat out to entrench themselves in.

If in one man a whole legion of devils have been billetted, how many hundred thousand legions retain to a term in London? If I said but to a tavern, it were an infinite thing. In Westminster Hall a man can scarce breathe for them; for in every corner they hover as thick as motes in the sun.

The Druids that dwelt in the Isle of Man, which are famous for great conjurers, are reported to have been lousy with familiars. Had they but put their finger and their thumb into their neck, they could have plucked out a whole nest of them.

There be them that think every spark in a flame is a spirit, and that the worms which at sea eat through a ship are so also; which may very well be, for have not you seen one spark of fire burn a whole town and a man with a spark of lightning made blind or killed outright? It is impossible the guns should go off as they do, if there were not a spirit either in the fire or in the powder.

Now for worms: what makes a dog run mad but a worm in his tongue? And what should that worm be but a spirit? Is there any reason such small vermin as they are should devour such a vast thing as a ship, or have the teeth to gnaw through iron and wood? No, no, they are spirits, or else it were incredible.

THOMAS NASHE,
from *The Terrors of the Night or A Discourse of Apparitions*

A Memorable Fancy

An Angel came to me and said: 'O pitiable foolish young man! O horrible! O dreadful state! consider the hot burning dungeon thou art preparing for thyself to all eternity, to which thou art going in such career.'

I said: 'perhaps you will be willing to shew me my eternal lot & we will contemplate together upon it and see whether your lot or mine is most desirable.'

So he took me thro' a stable & thro' a church & down into the church vault, at the end of which was a mill: thro' the mill we went, and came to a cave: down the winding cavern we groped our tedious way, till a void boundless as a nether sky appear'd beneath us, & we held by the roots of trees and hung over this immensity; but I said: 'if you please, we will commit ourselves to this void, and see whether providence is here also: if you will not, I will?' but he answer'd: 'do not presume, O young-man, but as we here remain, behold thy lot which will soon appear when the darkness passes away.'

So I remain'd with him, sitting in the twisted roof of an oak; he was suspended in a fungus, which hung with the head downward into the deep.

By degrees we beheld the infinite Abyss, fiery as the smoke of a burning city; beneath us, at an immense distance, was the sun, black but shining; round it were fiery tracks on which revolv'd vast spiders, crawling after their prey, which flew, or rather swum, in the infinite deep, in the most terrific shapes of animals sprung from corruption; & the air was full of them, & seem'd composed of them: these are Devils, and are called Powers of the air. I now asked my companion which was my eternal lot? He said: 'between the black & white spiders.'

But now, from between the black & white spiders, a cloud and fire burst and rolled thro' the deep, black'ning all beneath, so that the nether deep grew black as a sea, & rolled with a terrible noise; beneath us was nothing now to be seen but a black tempest, till looking east between the clouds & the waves, we saw a cataract of blood mixed with fire, and not many stones' throw from us appear'd and sunk again the scaly fold of a monstrous serpent; at last, to the east, distant about three degrees, appear'd a fiery crest above the waves; slowly it reared like a ridge of golden rocks, till we discover'd two globes of crimson fire, from which the sea fled away in clouds of smoke; and now we saw it was the head of Leviathan; his forehead was divided into streaks of green & purple like those on a tyger's forehead: soon we saw his mouth & red gills hang just above the raging foam, tinging the black deep with beams of blood, advancing toward us with all the fury of a spiritual existence.

My friend the Angel climb'd up from his station into the mill; I remain'd alone; & then this appearance was no more, but I found myself sitting on a pleasant bank beside a river by moonlight, hearing a harper, who sung to the harp; & his theme was: 'The man who never alters his opinion is like standing water, & breeds reptiles of the mind.'

But I arose and sought for the mill, & there I found my Angel, who, surprised, asked me how I escaped?

I answer'd: 'All that we saw was owing to your metaphysics; for when you ran away, I found myself on a bank by moonlight hearing a harper. But now we have seen my eternal lot, shall I shew you yours?' he laugh'd at my proposal; but I by force suddenly caught him in my arms, & flew westerly thro' the night, till we were elevated above the earth's shadow; then I flung myself with him directly into the body of the sun; here I clothed myself in white, & taking in my hand Swedenborg's volumes, sunk from the glorious clime, and passed all the planets till we came to saturn: here I staid to rest, & then leap'd into the void between saturn & the fixed stars.

'Here,' said I, 'is your lot, in this space, if space it may be call'd.' Soon we saw the stable and the church, & I took him to the altar and open'd the Bible, and lo! it was a deep pit, into which I descended, driving the Angel before me; soon we saw seven houses of brick; one we enter'd; in it were a number of monkeys, baboons, & all of that species, chain'd by the middle, grinning and snatching at one another, but witheld by the shortness of their chains: however, I saw that they sometimes grew numerous, and then the weak were caught by the strong, and with a grinning aspect, first coupled with, & then devour'd, by plucking off first one limb and then another, till the body was left a helpless trunk; this, after grinning & kissing it with seeming fondness, they devour'd too; and here & there I saw one savourily picking the flesh off of his own tail; as the stench terribly annoy'd us both, we went into the mill, & I in my hand brought the skeleton of a body, which in the mill was Aristotle's Analytics.

So the Angel said: 'thy phantasy has imposed upon me, & thou oughtest to be ashamed.'

I answer'd: 'we impose on one another, & it is but lost time to converse with you whose works are only Analytics.'

Opposition is true Friendship.

WILLIAM BLAKE,
from *The Marriage of Heaven and Hell*

The Pursuit

Lord! what a busy, restless thing
  Hast thou made man!
Each day, and hour he is on wing,
  Rests not a span;
Then having lost the sun, and light
  By clouds surprised
He keeps a commerce in the night
  With air disguised;
Hadst thou given to this active dust

  A state untired,
The lost son had not left the husk
  Nor home desired;
That was thy secret, and it is
  Thy mercy too,
For when all fails to bring to bliss,
  Then, this must do.
Ah! Lord! and what a purchase will that be
To take us sick, that sound would not take thee?

HENRY VAUGHAN

Hymn to Darkness

Thus when he first proclaim'd his sacred Law
 And would his *Rebel* subjects *awe*,
Like Princes on some great *solemnity*
H'appear'd in's *Robes of State*, and Clad himself with *thee*.

The Blest above do thy sweet *umbrage* prize,
    When *Cloy'd* with light, they *veil* their eyes.
The *Vision* of the Deity is made
More sweet and *Beatifick* by thy *Shade*.
But we poor *Tenants* of this Orb below
    Don't *here* thy excellencies know,
Till Death our understandings does *improve*,
And then our *Wiser ghosts* thy silent *night-walks* love.

But thee I *now* admire, thee would I chuse
    For my *Religion*, or my *Muse*.
'Tis hard to tell whether thy reverend shade
Has more good *Votaries* or *Poets* made,
From thy *dark Caves* were *Inspirations* given,
        And from thick *groves* went *vows* to Heaven.
Hail then thou *Muse's* and *Devotions* Spring,
'Tis *just* we should *adore*, 'tis *just* we should thee *sing*.

Hail thou most *sacred Venerable* thing,
    What Muse is worthy thee to sing?
Thee, from whose *pregnant universal* womb
All things, even *Light* thy *Rival*, first did Come.
What dares he not attempt that sings of thee,
    Thou *First* and greatest *Mystery*.
Who can the *Secrets* of thy essence tell?
Thou like the *light* of God art *inaccessible*.

Before *Great Love* this *Monument* did raise,
    This ample *Theater* of *Praise*.
Before the *folding Circles* of the Skie
Were *tuned* by him who is all *Harmony*.

Before the Morning Stars their *Hymn* began,
    Before the *Councel* held for *Man*,
Before the *birth* of either *Time* or *Place*,
Thou reign'st *unquestioned* Monarch in the *empty* Space.

Thy *native* lot thou didst to *light resign*,
    But still *half* of the Globe is *thine*.
Here with a *quiet*, but yet *aweful* hand,
Like the *best* Emperours thou dost command.
To thee the Stars *above* their *brightness* owe,
    And mortals their *repose below*,
To thy protection *Fear* and *Sorrow* flee,
And those that *weary* are of *light*, find *rest* in *thee*.

Tho *Light* and *Glory* be th'Almighty's *Throne*,
    Darkness is his *Pavilion*.
From that his radiant *Beauty*, but from thee
He has his *Terrour* and his *Majesty*.

JOHN NORRIS OF BEMERTON

Evensong

The Day is spent, and hath his will on me:
    I and the Sun have run our races,
    I went the slower, yet more paces,
        For I decay, not he.

Lord make my losses up, and set me free:
    That I who cannot now by day
    Look on his daring brightness, may
        Shine then more bright than he.

If thou defer this light, then shadow me:
   Lest that the Night, earth's gloomy shade,
   Fouling her nest, my earth invade,
      As if shades knew not Thee.

But Thou art Light and Darkness both together:
   If that be dark we cannot see:
   The sun is darker than a Tree,
      And thou more dark than either.

Yet Thou art not so dark, since I know this,
   But that my darkness may touch thine:
   And hope, that may teach it to shine,
      Since Light thy Darkness is.

O let my Soul, whose keys I must deliver
   Into the hands of senseless Dreams
   Which know not thee, suck in thy beams
      And wake with thee for ever.

GEORGE HERBERT

'Like as the waves make towards the pebbled shore'

Like as the waves make towards the pebbled shore,
So do our minutes hasten to their end;
Each changing place with that which goes before,
In sequent toil all forwards do contend.
Nativity, once in the main of light,
Crawls to maturity, wherewith being crowned,
Crookèd eclipses 'gainst his glory fight,
And Time that gave doth now his gift confound.

Time doth transfix the flourish set on youth,
And delves the parallels in beauty's brow,
Feeds on the rarities of nature's truth,
And nothing stands but for his scythe to mow.
    And yet to times in hope my verse shall stand,
    Praising thy worth, despite his cruel hand.

WILLIAM SHAKESPEARE

On the Beach at Night Alone

On the beach at night alone,
As the old mother sways her to and fro singing her husky
    song,
As I watch the bright stars shining, I think a thought of the clef
    of the universes and of the future.

A vast similitude interlocks all,
All spheres, grown, ungrown, small, large, suns, moons,
    planets,
All distances of place however wide,
All distances of time, all inanimate forms,
All souls, all living bodies though they be ever so different, or
    in different worlds,
All gaseous, watery, vegetable, mineral processes, the fishes,
    the brutes,
All nations, colors, barbarisms, civilizations, languages,
All identities that have existed or may exist on this globe, or
    any globe,
All lives and deaths, all of the past, present, future,

This vast similitude spans them, and always has spann'd,
And shall forever span them and compactly hold and enclose
   them.

WALT WHITMAN

The Terrors of Opium

I know not whether my reader is aware that many children,
perhaps most, have a power of painting, as it were, upon the
darkness, all sorts of phantoms: in some, that power is simply
a mechanic affection of the eye; others have a voluntary, or a
semi-voluntary power to dismiss or to summon them; or, as a
child once said to me when I questioned him on this matter, 'I
can tell them to go, and they go; but sometimes they come,
when I don't tell them to come.' Whereupon I told him that
he had almost as unlimited a command over apparitions, as a
Roman centurion over his soldiers. – In the middle of 1817, I
think it was, that this faculty became positively distressing to
me: at night, when I lay awake in bed, vast processions passed
along in mournful pomp; friezes of never-ending stories, that
to my feelings were as sad and solemn as if they were stories
drawn from times before Œdipus or Priam – before Tyre –
before Memphis. And, at the same time, a corresponding change
took place in my dreams; a theatre seemed suddenly opened and
lighted up within my brain, which presented nightly spectacles of
more than earthly splendour. And the four following facts may
be mentioned, as noticeable at this time:

1. That, as the creative state of the eye increased, a sympathy
seemed to arise between the waking and the dreaming states of
the brain in one point – that whatsoever I happened to call up
and to trace by a voluntary act upon the darkness was very apt
to transfer itself to my dreams; so that I feared to exercise this
faculty; for, as Midas turned all things to gold, that yet baffled

his hopes and defrauded his human desires, so whatsoever things capable of being visually represented I did but think of in the darkness, immediately shaped themselves into phantoms of the eye; and, by a process apparently no less inevitable, when thus once traced in faint and visionary colours, like writings in sympathetic ink, they were drawn out by the fierce chemistry of my dreams, into insufferable splendour that fretted my heart.

2. For this, and all other changes in my dreams, were accompanied by deep-seated anxiety and gloomy melancholy, such as are wholly incommunicable by words. I seemed every night to descend, not metaphorically, but literally to descend, into chasms and sunless abysses, depths below depths, from which it seemed hopeless that I could ever reascend. Nor did I, by waking, feel that I *had* reascended. This I do not dwell upon; because the state of gloom which attended these gorgeous spectacles, amounting at least to utter darkness, as of some suicidal despondency, cannot be approached by words.

3. The sense of space, and in the end, the sense of time, were both powerfully affected. Buildings, landscapes, &c. were exhibited in proportions so vast as the bodily eye is not fitted to receive. Space swelled, and was amplified to an extent of unutterable infinity. This, however, did not disturb me so much as the vast expansion of time; I sometimes seemed to have lived for 70 or 100 years in one night; nay, sometimes had feelings representative of a millennium passed in that time, or, however, of a duration far beyond the limits of any human experience.

4. The minutest incidents of childhood, or forgotten scenes of later years, were often revived: I could not be said to recollect them; for if I had been told of them when waking, I should not have been able to acknowledge them as parts of my past experience. But placed as they were before me, in dreams like intuitions, and clothed in all their evanescent circumstances and accompanying feelings, I *recognized* them instantaneously.

I was once told by a near relative of mine, that having in her childhood fallen into a river, and being on the very verge of death but for the critical assistance which reached her, she saw in a moment her whole life, in its minutest incidents, arrayed before her simultaneously as in a mirror; and she had a faculty developed as suddenly for comprehending the whole and every part. This, from some opium experiences of mine, I can believe; I have, indeed, seen the same thing asserted twice in modern books, and accompanied by a remark which I am convinced is true; viz. that the dread book of account, which the Scriptures speak of, is, in fact, the mind itself of each individual. Of this, at least, I feel assured, that there is no such thing as *forgetting* possible to the mind; a thousand accidents may, and will interpose a veil between our present consciousness and the secret inscriptions on the mind; accidents of the same sort will also rend away this veil; but alike, whether veiled or unveiled, the inscription remains for ever; just as the stars seem to withdraw before the common light of day, whereas, in fact, we all know that it is the light which is drawn over them as a veil – and that they are waiting to be revealed, when the obscuring daylight shall have withdrawn.

THOMAS DE QUINCEY,
from *Confessions of an English Opium Eater*

Songe 17

The Sunn is set, and masked night
vailes heavens fayer eyes.
Ah what trust is there to a light
that so swift flyes.

A new world doth his flames enjoy
New hartes rejoice.
In other eyes is now his joye
in other choice.

ROBERT SIDNEY,
EARL OF LEICESTER

'It is not, I confesse, an unlawfull Prayer'

It is not, I confesse, an unlawfull Prayer to desire to surpasse the dayes of our Saviour, or wish to out-live that age wherein he thought fittest to dye, yet, if (as Divinity affirmes) there shall be no gray hayres in Heaven, but all shall rise in the perfect state of men, we doe but out-live those perfections in this world, to be recalled unto them, by a greater miracle in the next, and run on here but to be retrograde hereafter. Were there any hopes to out-live vice, or a point to be super-annuated from sin, it were worthy our knees to implore the dayes of *Methuselah*. But age doth not rectifie, but incurvate our natures, turning bad dispositions into worser habits, and (like diseases) brings on incurable vices; for every day as we grow weaker in age, we grow stronger in sinne, and the number of our dayes doth but make our sinnes innumerable. The same vice committed at sixteene, is not the same, though it agree in all other circumstances, at forty, but swels and doubles from the circumstance of our ages, wherein besides the constant and inexcusable habit of transgressing, the maturity of our Judgement cuts off pretence unto excuse or pardon: every sin, the oftner it is committed, the more it acquireth in the quality of evill; as it succeeds in time, so it precedes in degrees of badnesse, for as they proceed they ever multiply, and like figures in Arithmeticke, the last stands for more than all that went before it: And though I thinke no man can live well once but hee that could live twice, yet for my owne part, I would not live over my houres past, or beginne againe the thred of my dayes: not upon *Cicero*'s ground, because I have lived them well, but for feare I should live them worse: I find my growing Judgement dayly instruct me how to be better, but my untaimed affections and confirmed vitiosity makes mee dayly doe worse; I finde in my confirmed age the same sinnes I discovered in my youth, I committed many then because I was a child, and because I commit them still I am yet an Infant. Therefore I perceive a man may bee twice a child before the dayes of dotage, and stand in need of Æsons bath before threescore.

SIR THOMAS BROWNE,
from *Religio Medici*

A Nocturnal Rêverie

In such a night, when every louder wind
Is to its distant cavern safe confined;
And only gentle zephyr fans his wings,
And lonely Philomel, still waking, sings;
Or from some tree, famed for the owl's delight,
She, hollowing clear, directs the wanderer right:
In such a night, when passing clouds give place,
Or thinly veil the heaven's mysterious face;
When in some river, overhung with green,
The waving moon and trembling leaves are seen;
When freshened grass now bears itself upright,
And makes cool banks to pleasing rest invite,
Whence springs the woodbind, and the bramble-rose,
And where the sleepy cowslip sheltered grows;
 Whilst now a paler hue the foxglove takes,
 Yet chequers still with red the dusky brakes:

When scattered glow-worms, but in twilight fine,
Show trivial beauties watch their hour to shine;
Whilst Salisbury stands the test of every light,
In perfect charms, and perfect virtue bright:
When odours, which declined repelling day,
Through temperate air uninterrupted stray;
When darkened groves their softest shadows wear,
And falling waters we distinctly hear;
When through the gloom more venerable shows
Some ancient fabric, awful in repose,
While sunburnt hills their swarthy looks conceal,
And swelling haycocks thicken up the vale:
When the loosed horse now, as his pasture leads,
Comes slowly grazing through the adjoining meads,
Whose stealing pace, and lengthened shade we fear,
Till torn up forage in his teeth we hear:
When nibbling sheep at large pursue their food,
And unmolested kine rechew the cud;
When curlews cry beneath the village-walls,
And to her straggling brood the partridge calls;
Their short-lived jubilee the creatures keep,
Which but endures, whilst tyrant-man does sleep:
When a sedate content the spirit feels,
And no fierce light disturbs, whilst it reveals;
But silent musings urge the mind to seek
Something, too high for syllables to speak;
Till the free soul to a composedness charmed,
Finding the elements of rage disarmed,
Over all below a solemn quiet grown,
Joys in the inferior world and thinks it like her own:

In such a night let me abroad remain,
Till morning breaks, and all's confused again;
Our cares, our toils, our clamours are renewed,
Or pleasures, seldom reached, again pursued.

ANNE, COUNTESS OF WINCHILSEA

'With how sad steps, O Moon, thou climb'st the skies'

With how sad steps, O Moon, thou climb'st the skies,
    How silently, and with how wan a face;
    What, may it be that e'en in heav'nly place
That busy archer his sharp arrows tries?
Sure, if that long-with-love-acquainted eyes
    Can judge of love, thou feel'st a lover's case;
    I read it in thy looks; thy languished grace,
To me that feel the like, thy state descries.
    Then e'en of fellowship, O Moon, tell me,
Is constant love deemed there but want of wit?
Are beauties there as proud as here they be?
Do they above love to be loved, and yet
    Those lovers scorn whom that love doth possess?
    Do they call virtue there ungratefulness?

SIR PHILIP SIDNEY

'Night is fallen within, without'

Night is fallen within, without
    Come, Love, soon!
I am weary of my doubt.
The golden fire of the Sun is out,
    The silver fire of the Moon.

Love shall be
A child in me
    When they are cinders gray,
With the earth and with the sea,
With the star that shines on thee,
    And the night and day.

MARY ELIZABETH COLERIDGE

An Exequy To his matchlesse never to be forgotten Freind

Accept thou Shrine of my Dead Saint,
Instead of Dirges this Complaint,
And for sweet flowres to crowne thy Hearse
Receive a strew of weeping verse
From thy griev'd Friend; whome Thou mightst see
Quite melted into Tears for Thee
    Deare Losse, since thy untimely fate
My task hath beene to meditate
On Thee, on Thee: Thou art the Book
The Library whereon I look

Though almost blind. For Thee (Lov'd Clay)
I Languish out, not Live the Day,
Using no other Exercise
But what I practise with mine Eyes.
By which wett glasses I find out
How lazily Time creepes about
To one that mournes: This, only This
My Exercise and bus'nes is:
So I compute the weary howres
With Sighes dissolved into Showres.

   Nor wonder if my time goe thus
Backward and most præposterous;
Thou hast Benighted mee. Thy Sett
This Eve of blacknes did begett
Who wast my Day (though overcast
Before thou hadst thy Noon-tide past)
And I remember must in teares,
Thou scarce hadst seene so many Yeeres
As Day tells Howres; By thy cleere Sunne
My Love and Fortune first did run;
But Thou wilt never more appeare
Folded within my Hemispheare:
Since both thy Light and Motion
Like a fledd Starr is fall'n and gone,
And 'twixt mee and my Soules deare wish
The Earth now interposed is,
Which such a straunge Ecclipse doth make
As ne're was read in Almanake.

   I could allow Thee for a time
To darken mee and my sad Clime,
Were it a Month, a Yeere, or Ten,
I would thy Exile live till then;
And all that space my mirth adjourne
So Thou wouldst promise to returne,

And putting on my dusty shrowd
At length disperse this Sorrowes Cloud.
   But woe is mee! the longest date
To narrowe is to calculate
These empty hopes. Never shall I
Be so much blest as to descry
A glympse of Thee, till that Day come
Which shall the Earth to cinders doome,
And a fierce Feaver must calcine
The Body of this World like Thine,
(My Little World!) That fitt of Fire
Once off, our Bodyes shall aspire
To our Soules blisse: Then wee shall rise,
And view our selves with cleerer eyes
In that calme Region, where no Night
Can hide us from each others sight.
   Meane time, thou hast Hir Earth: Much good
May my harme doe thee. Since it stood
With Heavens will I might not call
Hir longer Mine; I give thee all
My short liv'd right and Interest
In Hir, whome living I lov'd best.
With a most free and bounteous grief,
I give thee what I could not keep.
Be kind to Hir: and prethee look
Thou write into thy Doomsday book
Each parcell of this Rarity
Which in thy Caskett shrin'd doth ly:
See that thou make thy reck'ning streight,
And yeeld Hir back againe by weight.
For thou must Auditt on thy trust
Each Grane and Atome of this Dust,
As thou wilt answere Him that leant,
Not gave thee, my deare Monument.

So close the ground, and 'bout hir shade
Black Curtaines draw. My Bride is lay'd.

Sleep on my Love in thy cold bed
Never to be disquieted.

My last Good-night! Thou wilt not wake
Till I Thy Fate shall overtake:
Till age, or grief, or sicknes must
Marry my Body to that Dust
It so much loves; and fill the roome
My heart keepes empty in Thy Tomb.
Stay for mee there: I will not faile
To meet Thee in that hollow Vale.
And think not much of my delay,
I am already on the way,
And follow Thee with all the speed
Desire can make, or Sorrowes breed.
Each Minute is a short Degree,
And e'ry Howre a stepp towards Thee.
At Night when I betake to rest,
Next Morne I rise neerer my West
Of Life, almost by eight Howres sayle,
Then when Sleep breath'd his drowsy gale.

Thus from the Sunne my Bottome steares,
And my Dayes Compasse downward beares.
Nor labour I to stemme the Tide
Through which to Thee I swiftly glide.

Tis true with shame and grief I yield,
Thou like the Vann first took'st the Field,
And gotten hast the Victory
In thus adventuring to Dy
Before Mee; whose more yeeres might crave
A just præcedence in the Grave.
But hark! My Pulse like a soft Drum
Beates my Approach; Tells Thee I come;

And slowe howe're my Marches bee,
I shall at last sitt downe by Thee.
    The thought of this bids mee goe on
And wait my dissolution
With Hope and Comfort. Deare (forgive
The Crime) I am content to live
Divided, with but half a Heart,
Till wee shall Meet, and Never part.

HENRY KING

Evenèn in the Village

Now the light o' the west is a-turn'd to gloom,
    An' the men be at hwome vrom ground;
An' the bells be a-zendèn all down the Coombe
    From tower, their mwoansome sound.
        An' the wind is still,
        An' the house-dogs do bark,
An' the rooks be a-vled to the elems high an' dark,
    An' the water do roar at mill.

An' the flickerèn light drough the window-peäne
    Vrom the candle's dull fleäme do shoot,
An' young Jemmy the smith is a-gone down leäne,
    A-plaÿèn his shrill-vaïced flute.
        An' the miller's man
        Do zit down at his ease
On the seat that is under the cluster o' trees,
    Wi' his pipe an' his cider can.

WILLIAM BARNES

'Let's talk of graves, of worms, and epitaphs'

KING RICHARD: Let's talk of graves, of worms, and
    epitaphs;
Make dust our paper, and with rainy eyes
Write sorrow on the bosom of the earth.
Let's choose executors and talk of wills –
And yet not so; for what can we bequeath
Save our deposèd bodies to the ground?
Our lands, our lives, and all are Bolingbroke's,
And nothing can we call our own but death
And that small model of the barren earth
Which serves as paste and cover to our bones.
For God's sake let us sit upon the ground
And tell sad stories of the death of kings –
How some have been deposed, some slain in war,
Some haunted by the ghosts they have deposed,
Some poisoned by their wives, some sleeping killed,
All murdered. For within the hollow crown
That rounds the mortal temples of a king
Keeps death his court; and there the antic sits,
Scoffing his state and grinning at his pomp,
Allowing him a breath, a little scene,
To monarchize, be feared, and kill with looks,
Infusing him with self and vain conceit,
As if this flesh which walls about our life
Were brass impregnable; and humoured thus,
Comes at the last, and with a little pin
Bores through his castle wall, and – farewell, king!
Cover your heads, and mock not flesh and blood
With solemn reverence. Throw away respect,
Tradition, form, and ceremonious duty;

For you have but mistook me all this while.
I live with bread, like you; feel want,
Taste grief, need friends. Subjected thus,
How can you say to me I am a king?

WILLIAM SHAKESPEARE,
from *Richard II, III, 2*

The Lamp

'Tis dead night round about: horror doth creep
And move on with the shades; stars nod, and sleep,
And through the dark air spin a fiery thread
Such as doth gild the lazy glow-worm's bed.
    Yet, burn'st thou here, a full day; while I spend
My rest in cares, and to the dark world lend
These flames, as thou dost thine to me; I watch
That hour, which must thy life, and mine dispatch;
But still thou dost out-go me, I can see
Met in thy flames, all acts of piety;
Thy light, is *charity*; thy heat, is *zeal*;
And thy aspiring, active fires reveal
Devotion still on wing; then, thou dost weep
Still as thou burn'st, and the warm droppings creep
To measure out thy length, as if thou'dst know
What stock, and how much time were left thee now;
Nor dost thou spend one tear in vain, for still
As thou dissolv'st to them, and they distil,
They're stored up in the socket, where they lie,
When all is spent, thy last, and sure supply,
And such is true repentance, every breath
We spend in sighs, is treasure after death;

Only, one point escapes thee; that thy oil
Is still out with thy flame, and so both fail;
But whensoe'r I'm out, both shall be in,
And where thou mad'st an end, there I'll begin.

HENRY VAUGHAN

His Visitor

I come across from Mellstock while the moon wastes weaker
To behold where I lived with you for twenty years and more:
I shall go in the gray, at the passing of the mail-train,
And need no setting open of the long familiar door
      As before.

The change I notice in my once own quarters!
A formal-fashioned border where the daisies used to be,
The rooms new painted, and the pictures altered,
And other cups and saucers, and no cosy nook for tea
      As with me.

I discern the dim faces of the sleep-wrapt servants;
They are not those who tended me through feeble hours and
      strong,
But strangers quite, who never knew my rule here,
Who never saw me painting, never heard my softling song
      Float along.

So I don't want to linger in this re-decked dwelling,
I feel too uneasy at the contrasts I behold,
And I make again for Mellstock to return here never,
And rejoin the roomy silence, and the mute and manifold
      Souls of old.

THOMAS HARDY

Northern Wonders

In Iceland, as I have read and heard, spirits in the likeness of one's father or mother after they are deceased do converse with them as naturally as if they were living.

Other spirits like rogues they have among them, destitute of all dwelling and habitation, and they chillingly complain if a constable ask them *Chevala* in the night, that they are going unto Mount Hecla to warm them.

That Mount Hecla a number conclude to be hell mouth; for near unto it are heard such yellings and groans as Ixion, Titius, Sisyphus and Tantalus blowing all in one trumpet of distress could never conjoined bellow forth.

Bondmen in Turkey or in Spain are not so ordinarily sold as witches sell familiars there. Far cheaper may you buy a wind amongst them than you can buy wind or fair words in the Court. Three knots in a thread, or an odd grandam's blessing in the corner of a napkin will carry you all the world over.

We when we frown knit our brows, but let a wizard there knit a noose or a riding snarl on his beard, and it is hail, storm and tempest a month after.

More might be spoken of the prodigies this country sends forth, if it were not too much erring from my scope. Whole islands they have of ice, on which they build and traffic as on the mainland.

Admirable, above the rest, are the incomprehensible wonders

of the bottomless Lake Vether, over which no fowl flies but is frozen to death, nor any man passeth but he is senselessly benumbed like a statue of marble.

All the inhabitants round about it are deafened with the hideous roaring of his waters when the winter breaketh up, and the ice in his dissolving gives a terrible crack like to thunder, whenas out of the midst of it, as out of Mont-Gibell, a sulphureous stinking smoke issues, that wellnigh poisons the whole country.

A poison light on it, how come I to digress to such a dull, lenten, northern clime, where there is nothing but stock-fish, whetstones and cods' heads? Yet now I remember me: I have not lost my way so much as I thought, for my theme is the terrors of the night, and Iceland is one of the chief kingdoms of the night, they having scarce so much day there as will serve a child to ask his father blessing. Marry, with one commodity they are blest: they have ale that they carry in their pockets like glue, and ever when they would drink, they set it on fire and melt it.

It is reported that the Pope long since gave them a dispensation to receive the sacrament in ale, insomuch as, for their uncessant frosts there, no wine but was turned to red emayle as soon as ever it came amongst them.

Farewell, frost: as much to say as 'Farewell, Iceland', for I have no more to say to thee.

THOMAS NASHE,
from *The Terrors of the Night or
A Discourse of Apparitions*

from *A Sermon Preached at S. Pauls upon Easter-Day, 1630*

If I awake at midnight, and embrace God in mine armes, that is, receive God into my thoughts, and pursue those meditations, by such a having had God in my company, I may have frustrated many tentations that would have attempted me, and perchance prevailed upon me, if I had beene alone, for solitude is one of the devils scenes; and, I am afraid there are persons that sin oftner alone, than in company; but that man is not alone that hath God in his sight, in his thought. *Thou preventedst me with the blessings of goodnesse,* saies *David* to God. I come not early enough to God, if I stay till his blessings in a prosperous fortune prevent me, and lead me to God; I should come before that. *The dayes of affliction have prevented me,* saies *Job.* I come not early enough to God, if I stay till his Judgements prevent me, and whip me to him; I should come before that. But, if *I prevent the night watches, and the dawning of the morning,* If *in the morning my prayer prevent thee O God,* (which is a high expression of *Davids,* That I should wake before God wakes, and even prevent his preventing grace, before it be declared in any outward act, that day) If before blessing or crosse fall upon me, I surrender my selfe intirely unto thee, and say, Lord here I lye, make thou these sheets my sheets of penance, in inflicting a long sicknesse, or my winding sheete, in delivering me over to present death, Here I lye, make thou this bed mine Altar, and binde me to it in the cords of decrepitnesse, and bedridnesse, or throw me off of it into the grave and dust of expectation, Here I lye, doe thou choose whether I shall see any to morrow in this world, or begin my eternall day, this night, Thy Kingdome come, thy will be done.

JOHN DONNE

Inviting a Friend to Supper

To night, grave sir, both my poore house, and I
    Doe equally desire your companie:
Not that we thinke us worthy such a ghest,
    But that your worth will dignifie our feast,
With those that come; whose grace may make that seeme
    Something, which, else, could hope for no esteeme.
It is the faire acceptance, Sir, creates
    The entertaynment perfect: not the cates.
Yet shall you have, to rectifie your palate,
    An olive, capers, or some better sallade
Ushring the mutton; with a short-leg'd hen,
    If we can get her, full of egs, and then,
Limons, and wine for sauce: to these, a coney
    Is not to be despair'd of, for our money;
And, though fowle, now, be scarce, yet there are clarkes,
    The skie not falling, thinke we may have larkes.
Ile tell you of more, and lye, so you will come:
    Of partrich, pheasant, wood-cock, of which some
May yet be there; and godwit, if we can:
    Knat, raile, and ruffe too. How so ere, my man
Shall reade a piece of VIRGIL, TACITUS,
    LIVIE, or of some better booke to us,
Of which wee'll speake our minds, amidst our meate;
    And Ile professe no verses to repeate:
To this, if ought appeare, which I not know of,
    That will the pastrie, not my paper, show of.
Digestive cheese, and fruit there sure will bee;
    But that, which most doth take my *Muse*, and mee,
Is a pure cup of rich *Canary*-wine,
    Which is the *Mermaids*, now, but shall be mine:

Of which had HORACE, or ANACREON tasted,
   Their lives, as doe their lines, till now had lasted.
Tobacco, Nectar, or the *Thespian* spring,
   Are all but LUTHERS beere, to this I sing.
Of this we will sup free, but moderately,
   And we will have no *Pooly'*, or *Parrot* by;
Nor shall our cups make any guiltie men:
   But, at our parting, we will be, as when
We innocently met. No simple word,
   That shall be utter'd at our mirthfull boord,
Shall make us sad next morning: or affright
   The libertie, that wee'll enjoy to night.

BEN JONSON

On an Houre-glasse

My Life is measur'd by this glasse, this glasse
By all those little Sands that thorough passe.
See how they presse, see how they strive, which shall
With greatest speed and greatest quicknesse fall.
See how they raise a little Mount, and then
With their owne weight doe levell it agen.
But when th'have all got thorough, they give o're
Their nimble sliding downe, and move no more.
Just such is man whose houres still forward run,
Being almost finisht ere they are begun;
So perfect nothings, such light blasts are we,
That ere w'are ought at all, we cease to be.
Do what we will, our hasty minutes fly,
And while we sleep, what do we else but die?

How transient are our Joyes, how short their day!
They creepe on towards us, but flie away.
How stinging are our sorrows! where they gaine
But the least footing, there they will remaine.
How groundlesse are our hopes, how they deceive
Our childish thoughts, and onely sorrow leave!
How reall are our feares! they blast us still,
Still rend us, still with gnawing passions fill;
How senselesse are our wishes, yet how great!
With what toile we pursue them, with what sweat!
Yet most times for our hurts, so small we see,
Like Children crying for some Mercurie.
This gapes for Marriage, yet his fickle head
Knows not what cares waite on a Marriage bed.
This vowes Virginity, yet knowes not what
Lonenesse, griefe, discontent, attends that state.
Desires of wealth anothers wishes hold,
And yet how many have been choak'd with Gold?
This onely hunts for honour, yet who shall
Ascend the higher, shall more wretched fall.
This thirsts for knowledge, yet how is it bought?
With many a sleeplesse night and racking thought?
This needs will travell, yet how dangers lay
Most secret Ambuscado's in the way?
These triumph in their Beauty, though it shall
Like a pluck't Rose or fading Lillie fall.
Another boasts strong armes, 'las Giants have
By silly Dwarfes been drag'd unto their grave.
These ruffle in rich silke, though ne're so gay,
A well plum'd Peacock is more gay than they.
Poore man, what art! A Tennis ball of Errour,
A Ship of Glasse, toss'd in a Sea of terrour,

Issuing in blood and sorrow from the wombe,
Crauling in tears and mourning to the tombe,
How slippery are thy pathes, how sure thy fall,
How art thou Nothing when th'art most of all!

JOHN HALL

'Weary with toil, I haste me to my bed'

Weary with toil, I haste me to my bed,
The dear repose for limbs with travel tired;
But then begins a journey in my head
To work my mind when body's work's expired;
For then my thoughts, from far where I abide,
Intend a zealous pilgrimage to thee,
And keep my drooping eyelids open wide,
Looking on darkness which the blind do see;
Save that my soul's imaginary sight
Presents thy shadow to my sightless view,
Which like a jewel hung in ghastly night
Makes black night beauteous and her old face new.
  Lo, thus by day my limbs, by night my mind,
  For thee, and for myself, no quiet find.

WILLIAM SHAKESPEARE

'When I do count the clock that tells the time'

When I do count the clock that tells the time,
And see the brave day sunk in hideous night;
When I behold the violet past prime,
And sable curls all silvered o'er with white;
When lofty trees I see barren of leaves,
Which erst from heat did canopy the herd,
And summer's green, all girded up in sheaves,
Borne on the bier with white and bristly beard;
Then of thy beauty do I question make,
That thou among the wastes of time must go,
Since sweets and beauties do themselves forsake,
And die as fast as they see others grow;
    And nothing 'gainst Time's scythe can make defence
    Save breed to brave him when he takes thee hence.

WILLIAM SHAKESPEARE

'Not marble, nor the guilded monuments'

Not marble, nor the guilded monuments
Of Princes shall out-live this powrefull rime,
But you shall shine more bright in these contents
Then unswept stone, besmeer'd with sluttish time.
When wastefull warre shall *Statues* over-turne,
And broiles roote out the worke of masonry,
Nor *Mars* his sword, nor warres quick fire shall burne
The living record of your memory.

Gainst death, and all oblivious enmity
Shall you pace forth, your praise shall stil finde roome,
Even in the eyes of all posterity
That weare this world out to the ending doome.
    So til the judgement that your selfe arise,
    You live in this, and dwell in lovers eies.

WILLIAM SHAKESPEARE

'When to the sessions of sweet silent thought'

When to the sessions of sweet silent thought
I summon up remembrance of things past,
I sigh the lack of many a thing I sought,
And with old woes new wail my dear time's waste;
Then can I drown an eye, unused to flow,
For precious friends hid in death's dateless night,
And weep afresh love's long since cancelled woe,
And moan th'expense of many a vanished sight;
Then can I grieve at grievances foregone,
And heavily from woe to woe tell o'er
The sad account of fore-bemoanèd moan,
Which I new pay as if not paid before.
    But if the while I think on thee, dear friend,
    All losses are restored and sorrows end.

WILLIAM SHAKESPEARE

from *The City of Dreadful Night*

The city is not ruinous, although
  Great ruins of an unremembered past,
With others of a few short years ago
  More sad, are found within its precincts vast.
The street-lamps always burn; but scarce a casement
In house or palace front from roof to basement
  Doth glow or gleam athwart the mirk air cast.

The street-lamps burn amidst the baleful glooms,
  Amidst the soundless solitudes immense
Of rangèd mansions dark and still as tombs.
  The silence which benumbs or strains the sense
Fulfils with awe the soul's despair unweeping:
Myriads of habitants are ever sleeping,
  Or dead, or fled from nameless pestilence!

Yet as in some necropolis you find
  Perchance one mourner to a thousand dead,
So there; worn faces that look deaf and blind
  Like tragic masks of stone. With weary tread,
Each wrapt in his own doom, they wander, wander,
Or sit foredone and desolately ponder
  Through sleepless hours with heavy drooping head.

JAMES THOMSON

The Relapse

My God, how gracious art thou! I had slipped
      Almost to hell,
And on the verge of that dark, dreadful pit
      Did hear them yell,
But O thy love! thy rich, almighty love
      That saved my soul,
And checked their fury, when I saw them move,
      And heard them howl;
O my sole Comfort, take no more these ways,
      This hideous path,
And I will mend my own without delays,
      Cease thou thy wrath!
I have deserved a thick, Egyptian damp,
      Dark as my deeds,
Should *mist* within me, and put out that lamp
      Thy spirit feeds;
A darting conscience full of stabs, and fears;
      No shade but *yew*,
Sullen, and sad eclipses, cloudy spheres,
      These are my due.
But he that with his blood, (a price too dear,)
      My scores did pay,
Bid me, by virtue from him, challenge here
      The brightest day;
Sweet, downy thoughts; soft *lily*-shades; calm streams;
      Joys full, and true;
Fresh, spicy mornings; and eternal beams
      These are his due.

HENRY VAUGHAN

'I cannot tell how to say that fire is the essence of hell'

I cannot tell how to say that fire is the essence of hell, I know not what to make of Purgatory, or conceive a flame that can either prey upon, nor purifie the substance of a soule; those flames of sulphure mentioned in the Scriptures, I take not to be understood of this present Hell, but of that to come, where fire shall make up the complement of our tortures, & have a body or subject wherein to manifest its tyranny: Some who have had the honour to be textuarie in Divinity, are of opinion it shall be the same specificall fire with ours. This is hard to conceive, yet can I make good how even that may prey upon our bodies, and yet not consume us: for in this materiall world, there are bodies that persist invincible in the powerfullest flames, and though by the action of fire they fall into ignition and liquidation, yet will they never suffer a destruction: I would gladly know how *Moses* with an actuall fire calcin'd, or burnt the golden Calfe into powder: for that mysticall mettle of gold, whose solary and celestial nature I admire, exposed unto the violence of fire, grows onely hot and liquifies, but consumeth not: so when the consumable and volatile pieces of our bodies shall be refined into a more impregnable and fixed temper like gold, though they suffer from the action of flames, they shall never perish, but lie immortall in the armes of fire. And surely if this frame must suffer onely by the action of this element, there will many bodies escape, and not onely Heaven, but earth will not bee at an end, but rather a beginning; For at present it is not earth, but a composition of fire, water, earth, and aire; but at that time spoyled of these ingredients, it shall appeare in a substance more like it selfe, its ashes. Philosophers that opinioned the worlds destruction by fire, did never dreame of annihilation, which is beyond the power of sublunary causes;

for the last and proper action of that element is but vitrification or a reduction of a body into Glasse; & therefore some of our Chymicks facetiously affirm, that at the last fire all shall be crystallized & reverberated into glasse, which is the utmost action of that element. Nor need we fear this term 'annihilation' or wonder that God will destroy the workes of his Creation: for man subsisting, who is, and will then truely appeare a Microcosme, the world cannot bee said to be destroyed. For the eyes of God, and perhaps also of our glorified selves, shall as really behold and contemplate the world in its Epitome or contracted essence, as now it doth at large and in its dilated substance. In the seed of a Plant to the eyes of God, and to the understanding of man, there exists, though in an invisible way, the perfect leaves, flowers, and fruit thereof: (for things that are in *posse* to the sense, are actually existent to the understanding.) Thus God beholds all things, who contemplates as fully his workes in their Epitome, as in their full volume, and beheld as amply the whole world in that little compendium of the sixth day, as in the scattered and dilated pieces of those five before.

SIR THOMAS BROWNE,
from *Religio Medici*

The Mower to the Glo-Worms

Ye living Lamps, by whose dear light
The Nightingale does sit so late,
And studying all the Summer-night,
Her matchless Songs does meditate;

Ye Country Comets, that portend
No War, nor Princes funeral,
Shining unto no higher end
Then to presage the Grasses fall;

Ye Glo-worms, whose officious Flame
To wandring Mowers shows the way,
That in the Night have lost their aim,
And after foolish Fires do stray;

Your courteous Lights in vain you wast,
Since *Juliana* here is come,
For She my Mind hath so displac'd
That I shall never find my home.

ANDREW MARVELL

The Tombs in Westminster Abbey

Pallida mors aequo pulsat pede pauperum tabernas
    Regumque turres, o beate Sexti.
Vitae summa brevis spem nos vetat inchoare longam.
    Jam te premet nox, fabulaeque manes,
Et domus exilis Plutonia –   Horace

When I am in a serious humour, I very often walk by myself in
Westminster Abbey; where the gloominess of the place, and the
use to which it is applied, with the solemnity of the building,
and the condition of the people who lie in it, are apt to fill the
mind with a kind of melancholy, or rather thoughtfulness, that
is not disagreeable. I yesterday passed a whole afternoon in the
churchyard, the cloisters, and the church, amusing myself with
the tombstones and inscriptions that I met with in those several

regions of the dead. Most of them recorded nothing else of the buried person but that he was born upon one day and died upon another: the whole history of his life being comprehended in those two circumstances that are common to all mankind. I could not but look upon these registers of existence, whether of brass or marble, as a kind of satire upon the departed persons; who had left no other memorial of them, but that they were born and that they died. They put me in mind of several persons mentioned in the battles of heroic poems, who have sounding names given them for no other reason but that they may be killed, and are celebrated for nothing but being knocked on the head.

Γλαυκού τε Μεδοντὰ τε Θερσιλόχον τε. – HOM.
Glaucumque, Medontaque, Thersilochumque. – VIR.

The Life of these men is finely described in Holy Writ by the path of an arrow, which is immediately closed up and lost.

Upon my going into the church, I entertained myself with the digging of a grave; and saw in every shovelful of it that was thrown up, the fragment of a bone or skull intermixed with a kind of fresh mouldering earth that some time or other had a place in the composition of a human body. Upon this I began to consider with myself what innumerable multitudes of people lay confused together under that pavement of that ancient cathedral; how men and women, friends and enemies, priests and soldiers, monks and prebendaries, were crumbled amongst one another, and blended together in the same common mass; how beauty, strength, and youth, with old age, weakness, and deformity, lay undistinguished in the same promiscuous heap of matter.

After having thus surveyed this great magazine of mortality, as it were in the lump, I examined it more particularly by the accounts which I found on several of the monuments which are raised in every quarter of that ancient fabric. Some of them were covered with such extravagant epitaphs that, if it were possible for the dead person to be acquainted with them, he would blush at the praises which his friends have bestowed upon him. There are others so excessively modest that they deliver the character of the person departed in Greek or Hebrew, and by that means are not understood once in a twelve-month. In the poetical quarter, I found there were poets who had no monuments, and monuments which had no poets. I observed indeed that the present war had filled the church with many of these uninhabited monuments, which had been erected to the memory of persons whose bodies were perhaps buried in the plains of Blenheim, or in the bosom of the ocean.

I could not but be very much delighted with several modern epitaphs, which are written with great elegance of expression and justness of thought, and therefore do honour to the living as well as to the dead. As a foreigner is very apt to conceive an idea of the ignorance or politeness of a nation from the turn of their public monuments and inscriptions, they should be submitted to the perusal of men of learning and genius before they are put in execution. Sir Cloudesley Shovel's monument has very often given me great offence. Instead of the brave, rough English admiral, which was the distinguishing character of that plain, gallant man, he is represented on his tomb by the figure of a beau, dressed in a long periwig, and reposing himself upon velvet cushions under a canopy of state. The inscription is answerable to the monument, for instead of celebrating the many remarkable actions he had performed in the service of his country, it acquaints us only with the manner of his death, in which it was impossible for him to reap any honour. The Dutch, whom we are apt to despise for want of genius, show an infinitely greater taste of antiquity and politeness in their buildings and works of this nature, than what we meet with in those of our own country. The monuments of their admirals, which have been erected at the public expense, represent them like themselves, and are adorned with rostral crowns and naval ornaments, with beautiful festoons of seaweed, shells, and coral.

But to return to our subject, I have left the repository of our English kings for the contemplation of another day, when I shall find my mind disposed for so serious an amusement. I know that entertainments of this nature are apt to raise dark and dismal thoughts in timorous minds and gloomy imaginations; but for my own part, though I am always serious, I do not know what it is to be melancholy, and can therefore take a view of nature in her deep and solemn scenes, with the same pleasure as in her most gay and delightful ones. By this means, I can improve myself with those objects which others consider with terror. When I look upon the tombs of the great, every emotion of envy dies in me; when I read the epitaphs of the beautiful, every inordinate desire goes out; when I meet with the grief of parents upon a tombstone, my heart melts with compassion; when I see the tomb of the parents themselves, I consider the vanity of grieving for those whom we must quickly follow; when I see kings lying by those who deposed them, when I consider rival wits placed side by side, or the holy men that divided the world with their contests and disputes, I reflect with sorrow and astonishment on the little competitions, factions, and debates of mankind. When I read the several dates of the tombs – of some that died yesterday, and some six hundred years ago – I consider that great day when we shall all of us be contemporaries, and make our appearance together.

JOSEPH ADDISON

On the Tombs in
Westminster Abbey

Mortality, behold and fear
What a change of flesh is here!
Think how many royal bones
Sleep within these heaps of stones;
Here they lie, had realms and lands,
Who now want strength to stir their hands,
Where from their pulpits seal'd with dust
They preach, 'In greatness is no trust.'
Here's an acre sown indeed
With the richest royallest seed
That the earth did e'er suck in
Since the first man died for sin:
Here the bones of birth have cried
'Though gods they were, as men they died!'
Here are sands, ignoble things,
Dropt from the ruin'd sides of kings:
Here's a world of pomp and state
Buried in dust, once dead by fate.

FRANCIS BEAUMONT

'Come sleep, O sleep, the certain
knot of peace'

Come sleep, O sleep, the certain knot of peace,
The baiting place of wit, the balm of woe,
The poor man's wealth, the prisoner's release,
Th'indifferent judge between the high and low;

With shield of proof shield me from out the prease
Of those fierce darts despair at me doth throw:
O make in me those civil wars to cease;
I will good tribute pay if thou do so.

    Take thou of me smooth pillows, sweetest bed,
A chamber deaf to noise, and blind to light,
A rosy garland, and a weary head:
And if these things, as being thine by right,
      Move not thy heavy grace, thou shalt in me,
      Livelier than elsewhere, *Stella*'s image see.

SIR PHILIP SIDNEY

Three Meditations

The *Heavens* are not the less constant, because they move continually, because they move continually one and the same way. The *Earth* is not the more constant, because it lyes stil continually, because continually it changes, and melts in al the parts thereof. *Man*, who is the noblest part of the *Earth*, melts so away, as if he were a *statue*, not of *Earth*, but of *Snowe*. We see his owne *Envie* melts him, hee growes leane with that; he will say, anothers *beautie* melts him; but he feeles that a *Fever* doth not melt him like *snow*, but powr him out like lead, like yron, like brasse melted in a furnace: It doth not only *melt* him, but *Calcine* him, reduce him to *Atomes*, and to *ashes*; not to *water*, but to *lime*. And how quickly? Sooner than thou canst receive an answer, sooner than thou canst conceive the question; *Earth* is the *center* of my *Body*, *Heaven* is the *center* of my *Soule*; these two are the naturall places of those two; but those goe not to these two, in an equall pace: My *body* falls down without pushing, my *Soule* does not go up without pulling: *Ascension* is my *Soules* pace and measure, but *precipitation* my *bodies*: And, even *Angells*, whose home is *Heaven*, and who are winged too, yet had a *Ladder* to goe to *Heaven*, by steps. The *Sunne* who goes so many miles in a minut, The *Starres* of the *Firmament*, which goe so very many more, goe not so fast, as my *body* to the *earth*. In the same instant that I feele the first attempt of the disease, I feele the victory; In the twinckling of an eye, I can scarse see; instantly the tast is insipid, and fatuous; instantly the appetite is dull and desirelesse: instantly the knees are sinking and strengthlesse; and in an instant, sleepe, which is the picture, the copy of death, is taken away, that the *Originall, Death* it selfe may succeed, and that so I might have death to the life. It was part of *Adams* punishment, *In the sweat of thy browes thou shalt eate thy bread*: it is multiplied to me, I have earned bread in the sweat of my browes, in the labor of my calling, and I have it; and I sweat againe, and againe, from the brow, to the sole of the foot, but I eat no bread, I tast no sustenance: Miserable distribution of *Mankind*, where one halfe lackes meat, and the other stomacke.

It is too little to call *Man* a *little World*; Except *God*, Man is a *diminutive* to nothing. Man consistes of more pieces, more parts, than the world; than the world doeth, nay than the world is. And if those pieces were extended, and stretched out in Man, as they are in the world, Man would bee the *Gyant*, and the world the *Dwarfe*, the world but the *Map*, and the man the *World*. If all the *Veines* in our bodies, were extented to *Rivers*, and all the *Sinewes*, to *vaines of Mines*, and all the *Muscles*, that lye upon one another, to *Hilles*, and all the *Bones* to *Quarries* of stones, and all the other pieces, to the proportion of those which correspond to them in the *world*, the *aire* would be too litle for this *Orbe* of Man to move in, the firmament would bee but enough for this *star*; for, as the whole world hath nothing, to which something in man doth not answere, so hath man many pieces, of which the whol world hath no representation.

Inlarge this Meditation upon this *great world, Man,* so farr, as to consider the immensitie of the creatures this world produces; our *creatures* are our *thoughts, creatures* that are borne *Gyants*: that reach from *East* to *West,* from *earth* to *Heaven,* that doe not onely bestride all the *Sea,* and *Land,* but span the *Sunn* and *Firmament* at once; My thoughts reach all, comprehend all. Inexplicable mistery; I their *Creator* am in a close prison, in a sicke bed, any where, and any one of my *Creatures,* my *thoughts,* is with the *Sunne,* and beyond the *Sunne,* overtakes the *Sunne,* and overgoes the *Sunne* in one pace, one steppe, everywhere. And then as the other *world* produces *Serpents,* and *Vipers,* malignant, and venimous creatures, and *Wormes,* and *Caterpillars,* that endeavour to devoure that world which produces them, and *Monsters* compiled and complicated of divers parents, and kinds, so this world, our selves, produces all these in us, in producing *diseases,* and *sicknesses,* of all those sorts; venimous, and infectious diseases, feeding and consuming diseases, and manifold, and entangled diseases, made up of many several ones. And can the other world name so many *venimous,* so many consuming, so many monstrous creatures, as we can diseases, of all these kindes? O miserable abundance, O beggarly riches! how much doe wee lacke of having *remedies* for everie disease, when as yet we have not *names* for them? But wee have a *Hercules* against these *Gyants,* these *Monsters*; that is, the *Phisician*; hee musters up al the forces of the other world, to succour this; all Nature to relieve Man. We *have* the Phisician, but we *are not* the Phisician. Heere we shrinke in our proportion, sink in our dignitie, in respect of verie meane creatures, who are *Phisicians* to themselves. The *Hart* that is pursued and wounded, they say, knowes an Herbe, which being eaten, throwes off the arrow: A strange kind of *vomit.* The *dog* that pursues it, though hee bee subject to sicknes, even *proverbially,* knowes his *grasse* that recovers him. And it may be true, that the *Drugger* is as neere to *Man,* as to other *creatures,* it may be that obvious and present *Simples*, easie to bee had, would cure him; but the *Apothecary* is not so neere him, nor the *Phisician* so neere him, as they two are to other creatures; Man hath not that *innate instinct*, to apply those naturall medicines to his present danger, as those inferiour creatures have; he is not his owne *Apothecary*, his owne *Phisician*, as they are. Call back therefore thy Meditation again, and bring it downe; whats become of mans great extent and proportion, when himselfe shrinkes himselfe, and consumes himselfe to a handfull of dust; whats become of his soaring thoughts, his compassing thoughts, when himselfe brings himselfe to the ignorance, to the thought-lesnesse of the *Grave*? His *diseases* are his owne, but the *Phisician* is not; hee hath them at home, but hee must send for the Phisician.

This is *Natures nest of Boxes*; The Heavens containe the *Earth*, the *Earth*, *Cities*, *Cities*, *Men*. And all these are *Concentrique*; the common *center* to them all, is *decay*, *ruine*; only that is *Eccentrique*, which was never made; only that place, or garment rather, which we can *imagine*, but not *demonstrate*, That light, which is the very emanation of the light of *God*, in which the *Saints* shall dwell, with which the *Saints* shall be apparel'd, only that bends not to this *Center*, to *Ruine*, that which was not made of *Nothing*, is not threatened with this annihilation. All other things are; even *Angels*, even our *soules*; they move upon the same *poles*, they bend to the same *Center*; and if they were not made immortall by *preservation*, their *Nature* could not keepe them from sinking to this *center*, *Annihilation*. In all these (the *frame of the hevens*, the *States upon earth*, and *Men in them*, comprehend all) Those are the greatest mischifs, which are least discerned; the most insensible in their *wayes* come to bee the most sensible in their *ends*. The *Heavens* have had their *Dropsie*, they drownd the world, and they shall have their Fever, and burn the world. Of the *dropsie*, the flood, the world had a foreknowledge 120 yeares before it came; and so some made provision against it, and were saved; the *fever* shall break out in an instant, and consume all; The *dropsie* did no harm to the *heavens*, from whence it fell, it did not put out those *lights*, it did not quench those *heates*; but the *fever*, the fire shall burne the *furnace* it selfe, annihilate those *heavens*, that breath it out; Though the *Dog-Starre* have a pestilent breath, an infectious exhalation, yet because we know when it wil rise, we clothe our selves, and wee diet our selves, and we shadow our selves to a sufficient prevention; but *Comets* and *blazing starres*, whose effects, or significations no man can interrupt or frustrat, no man foresaw: no *Almanack* tells us, when a *blazing starre* will break out, the matter is carried up in secret; no *Astrologer* tels us when the effects wil be acomplished, for thats a secret of a higher spheare, than the other; and that which is most *secret*, is most *dangerous*. It is so also here in the *societies* of men, in *States*, and *Commonwealths*. Twentie *rebellious drums* make not so dangerous a noise, as a few *whisperers*, and secret plotters in corners. The *Canon* doth not so much hurt against a wal, as a *Myne* under the wall; nor a thousand enemies that threaten, so much as a few that take an *oath* to say *nothing*. *God* knew many heavy sins of the people, in the wilderness and after, but still he charges them with that one, with *Murmuring, murmuring* in their *hearts*, secret disobediences, secret repugnances against his declar'd wil; and these are the most deadly, the most pernicious. And it is so to, with the *diseases* of the *body*; and that is my case. The *pulses*, the *urine*, the *sweat*, all have sworn to say *nothing*, to give no *Indication* of any dangerous *sicknesse*. My forces are not enfeebled, I find no decay in my strength; my provisions are not cut off, I find no abhorring in mine appetite; my counsels are not corrupted or infatuated, I find no false apprehensions, to work upon mine understanding; and yet they see, that invisibly, and I feele, that insensibly the *disease* prevailes. The *disease* hath established a *Kingdome*, an *Empire* in mee, and will have certaine *Arcana Imperii, secrets of State*, by which it will proceed, and not be bound to *declare* them. But yet against those secret conspiracies in the State, the *Magistrate* hath the *rack*; and against these insensible diseases, *Phisicians* have their *examiners*; and those these employ now.

JOHN DONNE

Night

The sun descending in the west
The evening star does shine.
The birds are silent in their nest,
And I must seek for mine,
The moon like a flower,
In heavens high bower;
With silent delight,
Sits and smiles on the night.

Farewell green fields and happy groves,
Where flocks have took delight;
Where lambs have nibbled, silent moves
The feet of angels bright;
Unseen they pour blessing,
And joy without ceasing,
On each bud and blossom,
And each sleeping bosom.

They look in every thoughtless nest,
Where birds are covered warm;
They visit caves of every beast,
To keep them all from harm;

If they see any weeping,
That should have been sleeping
They pour sleep on their head
And sit down by their bed.

When wolves and tygers howl for prey
They pitying stand and weep;
Seeking to drive their thirst away,
And keep them from the sheep.
But if they rush dreadful;
The angels most heedful,
Recieve each mild spirit,
New worlds to inherit.

And there the lions ruddy eyes,
Shall flow with tears of gold:
And pitying the tender cries,
And walking round the fold:
Saying: wrath by his meekness
And by his health, sickness,
Is driven away,
From our immortal day.

And now beside thee bleating lamb,
I can lie down and sleep;
Or think on him who bore thy name,
Grase after thee and weep.
For wash'd in lifes river,
My bright mane for ever.
Shall shine like the gold.
As I guard o'er the fold.

WILLIAM BLAKE

The Pulley

When God at first made man,
Having a glass of blessings standing by,
Let us (said he) pour on him all we can:
Let the world's riches, which dispersed lie,
　　Contract into a span.

So strength first made a way;
Then beauty flowed, then wisdom, honour, pleasure:
When almost all was out, God made a stay,
Perceiving that alone of all his treasure
　　Rest in the bottom lay.

For if I should (said he)
Bestow this jewel also on my creature,
He would adore my gifts instead of me,
And rest in Nature, not the God of Nature:
　　So both should losers be.

Yet let him keep the rest,
But keep them with repining restlessness:
Let him be rich and weary, that at least,
If goodness lead him not, yet weariness
　　May toss him to my breast.

GEORGE HERBERT

Know Yourself

What am I? how produced? and for what end?
Whence drew I being? to what period tend?
Am I the abandoned orphan of blind chance,
Dropped by wild atoms in disordered dance?
Or from an endless chain of causes wrought?
And of unthinking substance, born with thought?
By motion which began without a cause,
Supremely wise, without design or laws.
Am I but what I seem, mere flesh and blood;
A branching channel, with a mazy flood?
The purple stream that through my vessels glides,
Dull and unconscious flows like common tides:
The pipes through which the circling juices stray,
Are not that thinking I, no more than they:
This frame, compacted, with transcendent skill,
Of moving joints obedient to my will;
Nursed from the fruitful glebe, like yonder tree,
Waxes and wastes: I call it mine, not me:
New matter still the mouldering mass sustains,
The mansion changed, the tenant still remains:
And from the fleeting stream repaired by food,
Distinct, as is the swimmer from the flood.
What am I then? sure, of a nobler birth.
Thy parent's right I own, O mother earth;
But claim superior lineage by my Sire,
Who warmed the unthinking clod with heavenly fire:
Essence divine, with lifeless clay allayed,
By double nature, double instinct swayed,
With look erect, I dart my longing eye,
Seem winged to part, and gain my native sky;

I strive to mount, but strive, alas! in vain,
Tied to this massy globe with magic chain.
Now with swift thought I range from pole to pole,
View worlds around their flaming centres roll:
What steady powers their endless motions guide,
Through the same trackless paths of boundless void!
I trace the blazing comet's fiery trail,
And weigh the whirling planets in a scale;
Those godlike thoughts, while eager I pursue,
Some glittering trifle offered to my view,
A gnat, an insect, of the meanest kind,
Erase the new-born image from my mind;
Some beastly want, craving, importunate,
Vile as the grinning mastiffs at my gate,
Calls off from heavenly truth this reasoning me,
And tells me I'm a brute as much as he.
If on sublimer wings of love and praise
My soul above the starry vault I raise,
Lured by some vain conceit, or shameful lust,
I flag, I drop, and flutter in the dust.
The towering lark thus from her lofty strain
Stoops to an emmet, or a barley grain.
By adverse gusts of jarring instincts tossed,
I rove to one, now to the other coast;
To bliss unknown my lofty soul aspires,
My lot unequal to my vast desires.
As 'mongst the hinds a child of royal birth
Finds his high pedigree by conscious worth,
So man, amongst his fellow brutes exposed,
Sees he's a king, but 'tis a king deposed.
Pity him, beasts! you by no law confined,
Are barred from devious paths by being blind;
Whilst man, through opening views of various ways,
Confounded, by the aid of knowledge strays;

Too weak to choose, yet choosing still in haste,
One moment gives the pleasure and distaste;
Bilked by past minutes, while the present cloy,
The flattering future still must give the joy.
Not happy, but amused upon the road,
And like you thoughtless of his last abode,
Whether next sun his being shall restrain
To endless nothing, happiness, or pain,
 Around me, lo, the thinking thoughtless crew,
(Bewildered each) their different paths pursue;
Of them I ask the way; the first replies,
Thou art a god; and sends me to the skies.
Down on this turf (the next) thou two-legged beast,
There fix thy lot, thy bliss, and endless rest;
Between those wide extremes the length is such,
I find I know too little or too much.
 'Almighty power, by whose most wise command,
Helpless, forlorn, uncertain here I stand;
Take this faint glimmering of thyself away,
Or break into my soul with perfect day!'
This said, expanded lay the sacred text,
The balm, the light, the guide of souls perplexed:
Thus the benighted traveller that strays
Through doubtful paths, enjoys the morning rays;
The nightly mist, and thick descending dew,
Parting, unfold the fields, the vaulted blue.
'O truth divine! enlightened by thy ray,
I grope and guess no more, but see my way;
Thou clear'dst the secret of my high descent,
And told me what those mystic tokens meant;
Marks of my birth, which I had worn in vain,
Too hard for worldly sages to explain;
Zeno's were vain, vain Epicurus' schemes,
Their systems false, delusive were their dreams;

Unskilled my twofold nature to divide,
One nursed by pleasure, and one nursed by pride;
Those jarring truths which human art beguile,
Thy sacred page thus bid me reconcile.'
Offspring of God, no less thy pedigree,
What thou once wert, art now, and still may be,
Thy God alone can tell, alone decree;
Faultless thou dropped from His unerring skill,
With the bare power to sin, since free of will;
Yet charge not with thy guilt His bounteous love;
For who has power to walk, has power to rove,
Who acts by force impelled, can nought deserve;
And wisdom short of infinite, may swerve.
Born on thy new-imped wings, thou took'st thy flight,
Left thy Creator, and the realms of light;
Disdained His gentle precept to fulfil;
And thought to grow a god by doing ill:
Though by foul guilt thy heavenly form defaced,
In nature changed, from happy mansions chased,
Thou still retain'st some sparks of heavenly fire,
Too faint to mount, yet restless to aspire;
Angel enough to seek thy bliss again,
And brute enough to make thy search in vain.
The creatures now withdraw their kindly use,
Some fly thee, some torment, and some seduce;
Repast ill-suited to such different guests,
For what thy sense desires, thy soul distastes;
Thy lust, thy curiosity, thy pride,
Curbed, or deferred, or balked, or gratified,
Rage on, and make thee equally unblessed
In what thou want'st, and what thou hast possessed;
In vain thou hop'st for bliss on this poor clod,
Return, and seek thy father, and thy God:

Yet think not to regain thy native sky,
Born on the wings of vain philosophy;
Mysterious passage! hid from human eyes;
Soaring you'll sink, and sinking you will rise:
Let humble thoughts thy wary footsteps guide,
Regain by meekness what you lost by pride.

JOHN ARBUTHNOT

'It is a beauteous evening, calm and free'

It is a beauteous evening, calm and free,
The holy time is quiet as a Nun
Breathless with adoration; the broad sun
Is sinking down in its tranquillity;
The gentleness of heaven broods o'er the Sea:
Listen! the mighty Being is awake,
And doth with his eternal motion make
A sound like thunder – everlastingly.
Dear Child! dear Girl! that walkest with me here,
If thou appear untouched by solemn thought,
Thy nature is not therefore less divine:
Thou liest in Abraham's bosom all the year;
And worshipp'st at the Temple's inner shrine,
God being with thee when we know it not.

WILLIAM WORDSWORTH

'Be absolute for death: either death or life'

DUKE: Be absolute for death: either death or life
   Shall thereby be the sweeter. Reason thus with life:
   If I do lose thee, I do lose a thing
   That none but fools would keep; a breath thou art,
   Servile to all the skyey influences
   That dost this habitation where thou keep'st
   Hourly afflict. Merely, thou art death's fool,
   For him thou labour'st by thy flight to shun,
   And yet runn'st toward him still. Thou art not noble,
   For all th'accommodations that thou bear'st
   Are nursed by baseness. Thou'rt by no means valiant,
   For thou dost fear the soft and tender fork
   Of a poor worm. Thy best of rest is sleep,
   And that thou oft provok'st, yet grossly fear'st
   Thy death, which is no more. Thou art not thyself,
      For thou exists on many a thousand grains
   That issue out of dust. Happy thou art not,
   For what thou hast not, still thou striv'st to get,
   And what thou hast, forget'st. Thou art not certain,
   For thy complexion shifts to strange effects,
   After the moon. If thou art rich, thou'rt poor,
   For, like an ass, whose back with ingots bows,
   Thou bear'st thy heavy riches but a journey,
   And death unloads thee. Friend hast thou none,
   For thine own bowels, which do call thee sire,
   The mere effusion of thy proper loins.
   Do curse the gout, serpigo, and the rheum
   For ending thee no sooner. Thou hast nor youth nor age,
   But as it were an after-dinner's sleep,
   Dreaming on both, for all thy blessed youth
   Becomes as agèd, and doth beg the alms

Of palsied eld: and when thou art old and rich,
Thou hast neither heat, affection, limb, nor beauty
To make thy riches pleasant. What's yet in this
That bears the name of life? Yet in this life
Lie hid more thousand deaths; yet death we fear,
That makes these odds all even.

WILLIAM SHAKESPEARE,
from *Measure for Measure*, III, 1

from *The Iliad VIII*

The Troops exulting sate in order round,
And beaming fires illumin'd all the ground.
As when the Moon, refulgent lamp of night!
O'er heav'ns clear azure spreads her sacred light,
When not a breath disturbs the deep serene,
And not a cloud o'ercasts the solemn scene;
Around her throne the vivid planets roll,
And stars unnumber'd gild the glowing pole,
O'er the dark trees a yellower verdure shed,
And tip with silver ev'ry mountain's head;
Then shine the vales, the rocks in prospect rise,
A flood of glory bursts from all the skies:
The conscious swains, rejoicing in the sight,
Eye the blue vault, and bless the useful light.
So many flames before proud *Ilion* blaze,
And lighten glimm'ring *Xanthus* with their rays.
The long reflections of the distant fires
Gleam on the walls, and tremble on the spires.
A thousand piles the dusky horrours gild,
And shoot a shady lustre o'er the field.

Full fifty guards each flaming pile attend,
Whose umber'd arms, by fits, thick flashes send.
Loud neigh the coursers o'er their heaps of corn,
And ardent warriors wait the rising morn.

ALEXANDER POPE

Dreaming

There is . . . a sort of profundity in sleep; and it may be usefully consulted as an oracle . . . It may be said, that the voluntary power is suspended, and things come upon us as unexpected revelations, which we keep out of our thoughts at other times. We may be aware of a danger, that yet we do not chuse, while we have the full command of our faculties, to acknowledge to ourselves: the impending event will then appear to us as a dream, and we shall most likely find it verified afterwards. Another thing of no small consequence is, that we may sometimes discover our tacit, and almost unconscious sentiments, with respect to persons or things in the same way. We are not hypocrites in our sleep. The curb is taken off from our passions, and our imagination wanders at will. When awake, we check these rising thoughts, and fancy we have them not. In dreams, we are off our guard, they return securely and unbidden. We may make this use of the infirmity of our sleeping metamorphosis, that we may repress any feelings of this sort that we disapprove in their incipient state, and detect, ere it be too late, an unwarrantable antipathy or fatal passion. Infants cannot disguise their thoughts from others; and in sleep we reveal the secret to ourselves.

It should appear that I have never been in love, for the same reason. I never dream of the face of anyone I am particularly attached to. I have thought almost to agony of the same person for years, nearly without ceasing, so as to have her face always before me and to be haunted by a perpetual consciousness of disappointed passion, and yet I never in all that time dreamt of this person more than once or twice, and then not vividly. I conceive, therefore, that this perseverance of the imagination in a fruitless track must have been owing to mortified pride, to an intense desire and hope of good in the abstract, more than to love, which I consider as an individual and involuntary passion, and which, therefore, when it is strong, must predominate over fancy in sleep. I think myself into love, and dream myself out of it. I should have made a very bad Endymion, in this sense; for all the time the heavenly Goddess was shining over my head, I should never have had a thought about her. If I had waked and found her gone, I might have been in a considerable *taking*. Coleridge used to laugh at me for my want of the faculty of dreaming; and once, on my saying that I did not like the preternatural stories in the Arabian Nights (for the comic parts I love dearly), he said, 'That must be because you never dream. There is a class of poetry built on this foundation, which is surely no inconsiderable part of our nature, since we are asleep and building up imaginations of this sort half our time.' I had nothing to say against it: it was one of his conjectural subtleties, in which he excels all the persons I ever knew . . .

WILLIAM HAZLITT,
from 'On Dreams'

'Hark, now every thing is still'

BOSOLA: Hark, now every thing is still,
  The screech-owl and the whistler shrill
  Call upon our Dame, aloud,
  And bid her quickly don her shroud.

Much you had of land and rent,
Your length in clay's now competent.
A long war disturb'd your mind,
Here your perfect peace is sign'd.
Of what is't fools make such vain keeping?
Sin their conception, their birth, weeping:
Their life, a general mist of error,
Their death, a hideous storm of terror.
Strew your hair with powders sweet:
Don clean linen, bathe your feet,
And, the foul fiend more to check,
A crucifix let bless your neck.
'Tis now full tide 'tween night and day,
End your groan, and come away.

JOHN WEBSTER,
from *The Duchess of Malfi*, IV, 2

Walking with God

Oh! for a closer walk with God,
   A calm and heavenly frame;
A light to shine upon the road
   That leads me to the lamb!

Where is the blessedness I knew
   When first I saw the Lord?
Where is the soul-refreshing view
   Of Jesus, and his word?

What peaceful hours I once enjoyed!
How sweet their memory still!
But they have left an aching void,
The world can never fill.

Return, o holy dove, return,
Sweet messenger of rest;
I hate the sins that made thee mourn,
And drove thee from my breast.

The dearest idol I have known,
Whate'er that idol be;
Help me to tear it from thy throne,
And worship only thee.

So shall my walk be close with God,
Calm and serene my frame;
So purer light shall mark the road
That leads me to the lamb.

WILLIAM COWPER

Tichborne's Elegy
*Written with his own hand in
the Tower before his execution.*

My prime of youth is but a froste of cares:
My feaste of joy, is but a dishe of payne:
My cropp of corne, is but a field of tares:
And all my good is but vaine hope of gaine:
The daye is gone, and yet I sawe no sonn:
And nowe I live, and nowe my life is donn

The springe is paste, and yet it hath not sprong
The frute is deade, and yet the leaves are greene
My youth is gone, and yet I am but yonge
I sawe the woorld, and yet I was not seene
My threed is cutt, and yet it was not sponn
And nowe I lyve, and nowe my life is donn.

I saught my death, and founde it in my wombe
I lookte for life, and sawe it was a shade.
I trode the earth and knewe it was my Tombe
And nowe I die, and nowe I am but made
The glasse is full, and nowe the glass is rune
And nowe I live, and nowe my life is donn

CHIDIOCK TICHBORNE

To the Moon

Art thou pale for weariness
Of climbing heaven, and gazing on the earth,
Wandering companionless
Among the stars that have a different birth, –
And ever-changing, like a joyless eye
That finds no object worth its constancy?

PERCY BYSSHE SHELLEY

Midnight

1

When to my eyes
(Whilst deep sleep others catches,)
Thine host of spies
The stars shine in their watches,
I do survey
Each busy ray,
And how they work, and wind,
And wish each beam
My soul doth stream,
With the like ardour shined;
What emanations,
Quick vibrations
And bright stirs are there?
What thin ejections,
Cold affections,
And slow motions here?

2

Thy heavens (some say),
Are a firy-liquid light,
Which mingling aye
Streams, and flames thus to the sight.
Come then, my god!
Shine on this blood,
And water in one beam,
And thou shalt see
Kindled by thee
Both liquors burn, and stream.
O what bright quickness,
Active brightness,

> And celestial flows
>   Will follow after
>   On that water,
> Which thy spirit blows!

HENRY VAUGHAN

From *The Complaint: or, Night-Thoughts on Life, Death and Immortality*

The bell strikes *one*: we take no note of time,
But from its loss. To give it then a tongue,
Is wise in man. As if an angel spoke,
I feel the solemn sound. If heard aright,
It is the knell of my departed hours;
Where are they? With the years beyond the flood:
It is the signal that demands dispatch;
How much is to be done? My hopes and fears
Start up alarmed, and o'er life's narrow verge
Look down – on what? a fathomless abyss;
A dread eternity! how surely mine!
And can eternity belong to me,
Poor pensioner on the mercies of an hour?

  How poor? how rich? how abject? how august?
How complicate? how wonderful is man?
How passing wonder He, who made him such?
Who centered in our make such strange extremes?
From different natures, marvelously mixed,
Connection exquisite of distant worlds!
Distinguished link in being's endless chain!
Midway from nothing to the Deity!
A beam ethereal sullied, and absorbed!

Though sullied, and dishonoured, still divine!
Dim miniature of greatness absolute!
An heir of glory! a frail child of dust!
Helpless immortal! Insect infinite!
A worm! a god! I tremble at myself,
And in myself am lost! at home a stranger,
Thought wanders up and down, surprised, amazed,
And wondering at her own: how reason reels?
O what a miracle to man is man,
Triumphantly distressed? what joy, what dread?
Alternately transported, and alarmed!
What can preserve my life? or what destroy?
An angel's arm can't snatch me from the grave;
Legions of angels can't confine me there.

EDWARD YOUNG

On Waking Early

There are few of us who have not sometimes wakened before
dawn, either after one of those dreamless nights that make us
almost enamoured of death, or one of those nights of horror
and misshapen joy, when through the chambers of the brain
sweep phantoms more terrible than reality itself, and instinct
with that vivid life that lurks in all grotesques, and that lends
to Gothic art its enduring vitality, this art being, one might
fancy, especially the art of those whose minds have been troubled
with the malady of reverie. Gradually white fingers creep through
the curtains, and they appear to tremble. In black fantastic
shapes, dumb shadows crawl into the corners of the room, and
crouch there. Outside, there is the stirring of birds among the
leaves, or the sound of men going forth to their work, or the
sigh and sob of the wind coming down from the hills, and

wandering round the silent house, as though it feared to wake the sleepers, and yet must needs call forth sleep from her purple cave. Veil after veil of thin dusky gauze is lifted, and by degrees the forms and colours of things are restored to them, and we watch the dawn remaking the world in its antique pattern. The wan mirrors get back their mimic life. The flameless tapers stand where we had left them, and beside them lies the half-cut book that we had been studying, or the wired flower that we had worn at the ball, or the letter that we had been afraid to read, or that we had read too often. Nothing seems to us changed. Out of the unreal shadows of the night comes back the real life that we had known. We have to resume it where we had left off, and there steals over us a terrible sense of the necessity for the continuance of energy in the same wearisome round of stereotyped habits, or a wild longing, it may be, that our eyelids might open some morning upon a world that had been refashioned anew in the darkness for our pleasure, a world in which things would have fresh shapes and colours, and be changed, or have other secrets, a world in which the past would have little or no place, or survive, at any rate, in no conscious form of obligation or regret, the remembrance even of joy having its bitterness, and the memories of pleasure their pain.

OSCAR WILDE,
from *The Picture of Dorian Gray*

Address to the Deil

O Prince, O chief of many throned pow'rs,
That led th' embattl'd Seraphim to war –

Milton

O Thou, whatever title suit thee!
Auld Hornie, Satan, Nick, or Clootie!
Wha in yon cavern grim an' sootie,
      Clos'd under hatches,
Spairges about the brunstane cootie,
      To scaud poor wretches!

Hear me, *auld Hangie*, for a wee,
An' let poor, *damned bodies* bee;
I'm sure sma' pleasure it can gie,
      Ev'n to a *deil*,
To skelp an' scaud poor dogs like me,
      An' hear us squeel!

Great is thy pow'r, an' great thy fame;
Far kend an' noted is thy name;
An' tho' yon *lowan heugh's* thy hame,
      Thou travels far;
An' faith! thou's neither lag nor lame,
      Nor blate nor scaur.

Whyles, ranging like a roaran lion,
For prey, a' holes an' corners tryin;
Whyles, on the strong-wing'd tempest flyin,
      Tirlan the *kirks*;
Whyles, in the human bosom pryin,
      Unseen thou lurks.

I've heard my rev'rend *Graunie* say,
In lanely glens ye like to stray;
Or where auld, ruin'd castles, gray,
                    Nod to the moon,
Ye fright the nightly wand'rer's way,
                    Wi' eldritch croon.

When twilight did my *Graunie* summon,
To say her prayers, douse, honest woman!
Aft 'yont the dyke she's heard you bumman,
                    Wi' eerie drone;
Or, rustling, thro' the boortries coman,
                    Wi' heavy groan.

Ae dreary, windy, winter night,
The stars shoot down wi' sklentan light,
Wi' you, *myself*, I gat a fright,
                    Ayont the lough;
Ye, like a *rass-buss*, stood in sight,
                    Wi' waving sugh.

The cudgel in my nieve did shake,
Each bristl'd hair stood like a stake,
When wi' an eldritch, stoor *quaick, quaick*,
                    Amang the springs,
Awa ye squatter'd like a *drake*,
                    On whistling wings.

Let *Warlocks* grim, an' wither'd *Hags*,
Tell how wi' you on ragweed nags,
They skim the muirs an' dizzy crags,
                    Wi' wicked speed;
And in kirk-yards renew their leagues,
                    Owre howcket dead.

Thence, countra wives, wi' toil an' pain,
May plunge an' plunge the *kirn* in vain;
For Oh! the yellow treasure's taen
   By witching skill;
An' dawtet, twal-pint *Hawkie's* gane
   As yell's the bill.

Thence, mystic knots mak great abuse,
On *Young-Guidmen*, fond, keen an' croose;
When the best *wark-lume* i' the house,
   By cantraip wit,
Is instant made no worth a louse,
   Just at the bit.

Then thowes dissolve the snawy hoord,
An' float the jinglan icy boord,
Then *water-kelpies* haunt the foord,
   By your direction,
An' nighted trav'llers are allur'd
   To their destruction.

An' aft your moss-traversing *spunkies*
Decoy the wight that late an' drunk is:
The bleezan, curst, mischievous monkies
   Delude his eyes,
Till in some miry slough he sunk is,
   Ne'er mair to rise.

When Mason's mystic *word* an' *grip*,
In storms an' tempests raise you up,
Some cock or cat, your rage maun stop,
   Or, strange to tell!
The *youngest brother* ye wad whip
   Aff straught to Hell.

Lang syne in Eden's bonie yard,
When youthfu' lovers first were pair'd,
An' all the Soul of Love they shar'd,
      The raptur'd hour,
Sweet on the fragrant, flow'ry swaird,
      In shady bow'r.

Then you, ye auld, snick-drawing dog!
Ye cam to Paradise incog,
An' play'd on man a cursed brogue,
      (Black be your fa'!)
An' gied the infant warld a shog,
      'Maist ruin'd a'.

D'ye mind that day, when in a bizz,
Wi' reeket duds, an' reestet gizz,
Ye did present your smoutie phiz,
      'Mang better folk,
An' sklented on the *man of Uzz*,
      Your spitefu' joke?

An how ye gat him i' your thrall,
An' brak him out o' house an' hal',
While scabs an' botches did him gall,
      Wi' bitter claw,
An' lows'd his ill-tongu'd, wicked *scrawl*
      Was warst ava?

But a' your doings to rehearse,
Your wily snares an' fechtin fierce,
Sin' that day Michael did you pierce,
      Down to this time,
Wad ding a *Lallan* tongue, or *Erse*,
      In Prose or Rhyme.

An' now, auld *Cloots*, I ken ye're thinkan,
A certain *Bardie's* rantin, drinkin,
Some luckless hour will send him linkan,
  To your black pit;
But faith! he'll turn a corner jinkan,
  An' cheat you yet.

But fare-you-weel, auld *Nickie-ben*!
O wad ye tak a thought an' men'!
Ye aiblens might – I dinna ken –
  Still hae a *stake* –
I'm wae to think upo' yon den,
  Ev'n for your sake!

ROBERT BURNS

'The number of those who pretend unto salvation'

The number of those who pretend unto salvation, and those
infinite swarmes who thinke to passe through the eye of this
Needle, have much amazed me. That name and compellation of
little Flocke, doth not comfort but deject my devotion, especially
when I reflect upon mine owne unworthinesse, wherein, according to my humble apprehensions, I am below them all. I beleeve
there shall never be an Anarchy in Heaven, but as there are
Hierarchies amongst the Angels, so shall there be degrees of
priority amongst the Saints. Yet is it (I protest) beyond my
ambition to aspire unto the first rankes, my desires onely are,
and I shall be happy therein, to be but the last man, and bring
up the Rere in Heaven.

SIR THOMAS BROWNE,
from Religio Medici

Night Fear

The glasses of our sight, in the night, are like the prospective
glasses one Hostius made in Rome, which represented the images
of things far greater than they were. Each mote in the dark they
make a monster, and every slight glimmering a giant.

A solitary man in his bed is like a poor bed-red lazar lying
by the highway-side unto whose displayed wounds and sores a
number of stinging flies do swarm for pastance and beverage.
His naked wounds are his inward heart-griping woes, the wasps
and flies his idle wandering thoughts; who to that secret smarting
pain he hath already do add a further sting of impatience and
new-lance his sleeping griefs and vexations.

THOMAS NASHE,
from *The Terrors of the Night or*
A Discourse of Apparitions

To Sleep

O soft embalmer of the still midnight,
    Shutting, with careful fingers and benign,
Our gloom-pleased eyes, embowered from the light,
    Enshaded in forgetfulness divine:
O soothest Sleep! if so it please thee, close
    In midst of this thine hymn, my willing eyes,
Or wait the 'Amen', ere thy poppy throws
    Around my bed its lulling charities.
Then save me, or the passèd day will shine
Upon my pillow, breeding many woes;
    Save me from curious conscience, that still hoards

Its strength for darkness, burrowing like the mole;
   Turn the key deftly in the oilèd wards,
And seal the hushèd casket of my soul.

JOHN KEATS

Limbo

'Tis a strange place, this Limbo! – not a Place,
Yet name it so; – where Time and weary Space
Fettered from flight, with night-mare sense of fleeing,
Strive for their last crepuscular half-being; –
Lank Space, and scytheless Time with branny hands
Barren and soundless as the measuring sands,
Not mark'd by flit of Shades, – unmeaning they
As moonlight on the dial of the day!
But that is lovely – looks like human Time, –
An old man with a steady look sublime,
That stops his earthly task to watch the skies;
But he is blind – a statue hath such eyes; –
Yet having moonward turn'd his face by chance,
Gazes the orb with moon-like countenance,
With scant white hairs, with foretop bald and high,
He gazes still, – his eyeless face all eye; –
As 'twere an organ full of silent sight,
His whole face seemeth to rejoice in light! –
Lip touching lip, all moveless, bust and limb –
He seems to gaze at that which seems to gaze on him!
   No such sweet sights doth Limbo den immure,
Wall'd round, and made a spirit-jail secure,
By the mere horror of blank Naught-at-all,
Whose circumambience doth these ghosts enthral.

A lurid thought is growthless, dull Privation,
Yet that is but a Purgatory curse;
Hell knows a fear far worse,
A fear – a future state; – 'tis positive Negation!

SAMUEL TAYLOR COLERIDGE

'Even suche is tyme that takes in trust'

Even suche is tyme that takes in trust
our youth, our joies and what we have
And paies us but with earth, and dust
which in the Darke and silent grave
when we have wandred all our waies
shutts up the storie of our daies:
    But from this earth, this grave this dust
    The Lord will raise me up I trust.

SIR WALTER RALEGH

The burning Babe

As I in hoarie Winters night stoode shivering in the snow,
Surpris'd I was with sodaine heate, which made my hart to
    glow;
And lifting up a fearefull eye, to view what fire was neare,
A pretty Babe all burning bright did in the ayre appeare;
Who scorched with excessive heate, such floods of tears did
    shed,
As though his floods should quench his flames, which with his
    teares were fed:

Alas (quoth he) but newly borne, in fierie heates I frie,
Yet none approach to warme their harts or feele my fire, but I;
My faultlesse breast the furnace is, the fuell wounding thornes:
Love is the fire, and sighs the smoake, the ashes, shame and
    scornes;
The fewell Justice layeth on, and Mercie blowes the coales,
The mettall in this furnace wrought, are mens defiled soules:
For which, as now on fire I am to worke them to their good,
So will I melt into a bath, to wash them in my blood.
With this he vanisht out of sight, and swiftly shrunk away,
And straight I called unto minde, that it was Christmasse day.

ROBERT SOUTHWELL

Ay Waukin, O

Simmer's a pleasant time,
Flow'rs of ev'ry colour;
The water rins o'er the heugh,
And I long for my true lover!

Ay waukin, O,
Waukin still and weary:
Sleep I can get nane,
For thinking on my Dearie.

When I sleep I dream,
When I wauk I'm irie;
Sleep I can get nane
For thinking on my Dearie.

Ay waukin &c.

Lanely night comes on,
A' the lave are sleepin:
I think on my bony lad
And I bleer my een wi' greetin.

Ay waukin &c.

ROBERT BURNS

The Collar

I struck the board, and cry'd, No more.
        I will abroad.
What? shall I ever sigh and pine?
My lines and life are free; free as the rode,
    Loose as the winde, as large as store.
            Shall I be still in suit?
    Have I no harvest but a thorn
    To let me bloud, and not restore
What I have lost with cordiall fruit?
            Sure there was wine
Before my sighs did drie it: there was corn
        Before my tears did drown it.
    Is the yeare onely lost to me?
        Have I no bayes to crown it?
No flowers, no garlands gay? all blasted?
            All wasted?
    Not so, my heart: but there is fruit,
            And thou hast hands.
        Recover all thy sigh-blown age
On double pleasures: leave thy cold dispute
Of what is fit, and not. Forsake thy cage,
            Thy rope of sands,

Which pettie thoughts have made, and made to thee
    Good cable, to enforce and draw,
        And be thy law,
While thou didst wink and wouldst not see.
      Away; take heed:
      I will abroad.
Call in thy deaths head there: tie up thy fears.
      He that forbears
    To suit and serve his need,
      Deserves his load.
But as I rav'd and grew more fierce and wilde
      At every word,
Me thoughts I heard one calling, *Childe*:
      And I reply'd, *My Lord*.

GEORGE HERBERT

'I wake and feel the fell of dark, not day'

I wake and feel the fell of dark, not day.
What hours, O what black hours we have spent
This night! what sights you, heart, saw; ways you went!
And more must, in yet longer light's delay.

    With witness I speak this. But where I say
Hours I mean years, mean life. And my lament
Is cries countless, cries like dead letters sent
To dearest him that lives alas! away.

    I am gall, I am heartburn. God's most deep decree
Bitter would have me taste: my taste was me;

Bones built in me, flesh filled, blood brimmed the curse.
  Selfyeast of spirit a dull dough sours. I see
The lost are like this, and their scourge to be
As I am mine, their sweating selves; but worse.

GERARD MANLEY HOPKINS

Guilt

There were gates in Rome out of which nothing was carried but dust and dung, and men to execution; so, many of the gates of our senses serve for nothing but to convey our excremental vapours and affrighting deadly dreams, that are worse than executioners unto us.

Ah, woe be to the solitary man that hath his sins continually about him, that hath no withdrawing place from the devil and his temptations.

Much I wonder how treason and murder dispense with the darkness of the night, how they can shrive themselves to it, and not rave and die. Methinks they should imagine that hell embraceth them round, when she overspreads them with her black pitchy mantle.

Dreams to none are so fearful, as to those whose accusing private guilt expects mischief every hour for their merit. Wonderful superstitious are such persons in observing every accident that befalls them; and that their superstition is as good as an hundred furies to torment them. Never in this world shall he enjoy one quiet day, that once hath given himself over to be her slave. His ears cannot glow, his nose itch, or his eyes smart, but his destiny stands upon her trial, and till she be acquitted or condemned he is miserable.

A cricket or a raven keep him forty times in more awe than God or the devil.

If he chance to kill a spider, he hath suppressed an enemy; if a spinner creep upon him, he shall have gold rain down from heaven. If his nose bleed, some of his kinsfolks is dead; if the salt fall right against him, all the stars cannot save him from some immediate misfortune.

THOMAS NASHE,
from *The Terrors of the Night or
A Discourse of Apparitions*

Lines Inscribed upon a Cup Formed from a Skull

Start not – nor deem my spirit fled;
  In me behold the only skull,
From which, unlike a living head,
  Whatever flows is never dull.

I lived, I loved, I quaff'd, like thee:
  I died: let earth my bones resign;
Fill up – thou canst not injure me;
  The worm hath fouler lips than thine.

Better to hold the sparkling grape,
  Than nurse the earth-worm's slimy brood;
And circle in the goblet's shape
  The drink of gods, than reptile's food.

Where once my wit, perchance, hath shone,
  In aid of others' let me shine;
And when, alas! our brains are gone,
  What nobler substitute than wine?

Quaff while thou canst: another race,
   When thou and thine, like me, are sped,
May rescue thee from earth's embrace,
   And rhyme and revel with the dead.

Why not? since through life's little day
   Our heads such sad effects produce;
Redeem'd from worms and wasting clay,
   This chance is theirs, to be of use.

GEORGE GORDON, LORD BYRON

'Devouring time blunt thou the Lyons pawes'

Devouring time blunt thou the Lyons pawes,
And make the earth devoure her owne sweet brood,
Plucke the keene teeth from the fierce Tygers yawes,
And burne the long liv'd Phænix in her blood,
Make glad and sorry seasons as thou fleet'st,
And do what ere thou wilt swift-footed time
To the wide world and all her fading sweets:
But I forbid thee one most hainous crime,
O carve not with thy howers my loves faire brow,
Nor draw noe lines there with thine antique pen,
Him in thy course untainted doe allow,
For beauties patterne to succeding men.
   Yet doe thy worst ould Time; dispight thy wrong,
   My love shall in my verse ever live young.

WILLIAM SHAKESPEARE

A Belmans Song

Maides to bed, and cover coale,
Let the Mouse Out of her hole:
Crickets in the Chimney sing,
Whil'st the little Bell doth ring.
If fast asleepe, who can tell
When the Clapper hits the Bell.

THOMAS RAVENSCROFT

'Over the dark world flies the wind'

Over the dark world flies the wind
    And clatters in the sapless trees,
From cloud to cloud thro' darkness blind
    Quick stars scud o'er the sounding seas:
I look: the showery skirts unbind:
    Mars by the lonely Pleiades
Burns overhead: with brows declined
    I muse – I wander from my peace,
And still divide the rapid mind
    This way and that in search of ease.

ALFRED LORD TENNYSON

On the Beach at Night

On the beach at night,
Stands a child with her father,
Watching the east, the autumn sky.

Up through the darkness,
While ravening clouds, the burial clouds, in black masses
    spreading,
Lower sullen and fast athwart and down the sky,
Amid a transparent clear belt of ether yet left in the east,
Ascends large and calm the lord-star Jupiter,
And nigh at hand, only a very little above,
Swim the delicate sisters the Pleiades.

From the beach the child holding the hand of her father,
Those burial-clouds that lower victorious soon to devour all,
Watching, silently weeps.

Weep not, my child,
Weep not, my darling,
With these kisses let me remove your tears,
The ravening clouds shall not long be victorious,
They shall not long possess the sky, they devour the stars only
    in apparition,
Jupiter shall emerge, be patient, watch again another night, the
    Pleiades shall emerge,
They are immortal, all those stars both silvery and golden shall
    shine out again,
The great stars and the little ones shall shine out again, they
    endure,
The vast immortal suns and the long-enduring pensive moons
    shall again shine.

Then dearest child mournest thou only for Jupiter?
Considerest thou alone the burial of the stars?

Something there is,
(With my lips soothing thee, adding I whisper,
I give thee the first suggestion, the problem and indirection,)
Something there is more immortal even than the stars,
(Many the burials, many the days and nights, passing away,)
Something that shall endure longer even than lustrous Jupiter,
Longer than sun or any revolving satellite,
Or the radiant sisters the Pleiades.

WALT WHITMAN

A Summer Night

In the deserted, moon-blanch'd street,
How lonely rings the echo of my feet!
Those windows, which I gaze at, frown,
Silent and white, unopening down,
Repellent as the world; – but see,
A break between the housetops shows
The moon! and, lost behind her, fading dim
Into the dewy dark obscurity
Down at the far horizon's rim,
Doth a whole tract of heaven disclose!

And to my mind the thought
Is on a sudden brought
Of a past night, and a far different scene.
Headlands stood out into the moonlit deep
As clearly as at noon;
The spring-tide's brimming flow

Heaved dazzlingly between;
Houses, with long white sweep,
Girdled the glistening bay;
Behind, through the soft air,
The blue haze-cradled mountains spread away,
The night was far more fair –
But the same restless pacings to and fro,
And the same vainly throbbing heart was there,
And the same bright, calm moon.

And the calm moonlight seems to say:
Hast thou then still the old unquiet breast,
Which neither deadens into rest,
Nor ever feels the fiery glow
That whirls the spirit from itself away,
But fluctuates to and fro,
Never by passion quite possess'd
And never quite benumb'd by the world's sway? –
And I, I know not if to pray
Still to be what I am, or yield and be
Like all the other men I see.

For most men in a brazen prison live,
Where, in the sun's hot eye,
With heads bent o'er their toil, they languidly
Their lives to some unmeaning taskwork give,
Dreaming of nought beyond their prison-wall.
And as, year after year,
Fresh products of their barren labour fall
From their tired hands, and rest
Never yet comes more near,
Gloom settles slowly down over their breast;

And while they try to stem
The waves of mournful thought by which they are prest
Death in their prison reaches them,
Unfreed, having seen nothing, still unblest.

And the rest, a few,
Escape their prison and depart
On the wide ocean of life anew.
There the freed prisoner, where'er his heart
Listeth, will sail;
Nor doth he know how there prevail,
Despotic on that sea,
Trade-winds which cross it from eternity.
Awhile he holds some false way, undebarr'd
By thwarting signs, and braves
The freshening wind and blackening waves.
And then the tempest strikes him; and between
The lightning-bursts is seen
Only a driving wreck,
And the pale master on his spar-strewn deck
With anguish'd face and flying hair
Grasping the rudder hard,
Still bent to make some port he knows not where,
Still standing for some false, impossible shore.
And sterner comes the roar
Of sea and wind, and through the deepening gloom
Fainter and fainter wreck and helmsman loom,
And he too disappears, and comes no more.

Is there no life, but these alone?
Madman or slave, must man be one?

Plainness and clearness without shadow of stain!
Clearness divine!
Ye heavens, whose pure dark regions have no sign
Of languor, though so calm, and, though so great,
Are yet untroubled and unpassionate;
Who, though so noble, share in the world's toil,
And, though so task'd, keep free from dust and soil!
I will not say that your mild deeps retain
A tinge, it may be, of their silent pain
Who have long'd deeply once, and long'd in vain –
But I will rather say that you remain
A world above man's head, to let him see
How boundless might his soul's horizons be,
How vast, yet of what clear transparency!
How it were good to abide there, and breathe free;
How fair a lot to fill
Is left to each man still!

MATTHEW ARNOLD

Faustus Summons Mephostophilis

Thunder. Enter LUCIFER *and* FOUR DEVILS.
FAUSTUS *to them with this speech.*
FAUSTUS: Now that the gloomy shadow of the night,
   Longing to view Orion's drizzling look,
   Leaps from th'Antarctick world unto the sky,
   And dims the Welkin with her pitchy breath,
   Faustus, begin thine incantations
   And try if devils will obey thy hest,
   Seeing thou hast prayed and sacrificed to them.
   Within this circle is Jehova's name
   Forward and backward anagrammatised:
   The abbreviated names of holy saints,

Figures of every adjunct to the heavens,
And characters of signs and evening stars,
By which the spirits are enforced to rise.
Then fear not, Faustus, to be resolute
And try the utmost magic can perform.

Thunder.

Sint mihi dei acherontis propitii, valeat numen triplex Jehovae, ignei areii, aquatani spiritus salvete: orientis princeps Belzebub, inferni ardentis monarcha et demigorgon, propitiamus vos, ut appareat, et surgat Mephostophilis quod tumeraris: per Jehovam, gehennam, et consecratam aquam quam nunc spargo; signumque crucis quod nunc facio; et per vota nostra ipse nunc surgat nobis dicatus Mephostophilis.

[May the gods of the underworld (Acheron) be kind to me; may the triple deity of Jehovah be gone; to the spirits of fire, air and water, greetings. Prince of the east, Beelzebub, monarch of the fires below, and Demogorgon, we appeal to you so that Mephostophilis may appear and rise. Why do you delay (*Quod tu moraris*)? By Jehovah, hell and the hallowed water which I now sprinkle, and the sign of the cross, which I now make, and by our vows, let Mephostophilis himself now arise to serve us.]

Enter a DEVIL.

I charge thee to return and change thy shape.
Thou art too ugly to attend on me.
Go, and return an old Franciscan friar:
That holy shape becomes a devil best.

Exit DEVIL.

I see there's virtue in my heavenly words.
Who would not be proficient in this art?
How pliant is this Mephostophilis!
Full of obedience and humility,
Such is the force of magic and my spells.

Now, Faustus, thou art conjuror laureate:
Thou canst command great Mephostophilis.
Quin redis Mephostophilis fratris imagine
[Why do you not return, Mephostophilis, in the appear-
 ance of a friar?]
Enter MEPHOSTOPHILIS.

MEPHOSTOPHILIS: Now, Faustus, what wouldst thou have
 me do?

FAUSTUS: I charge thee wait upon me whilst I live,
 To do whatever Faustus shall command,
 Be it to make the moon drop from her sphere,
 Or the ocean to overwhelm the world.

MEPHOSTOPHILIS: I am a servant to great Lucifer,
 And may not follow thee without his leave.
 No more than he commands must we perform.

FAUSTUS: Did not he charge thee to appear to me?

MEPHOSTOPHILIS: No, I came now hither of mine own
 accord.

FAUSTUS: Did not my conjuring speeches raise thee? Speak.

MEPHOSTOPHILIS: That was the cause, but yet *per accidens*;
 For when we hear one rack the name of God,
 Abjure the scriptures and his saviour Christ,
 We fly in hope to get his glorious soul.
 Nor will we come unless he use such means
 Whereby he is in danger to be damned.
 Therefore the shortest cut for conjuring
 Is stoutly to abjure all godliness
 And pray devoutly to the prince of hell.

FAUSTUS: So Faustus hath already done, and holds this
 principle:
 There is no chief but only Belzebub,
 To whom Faustus doth dedicate himself.
 This word 'damnation' terrifies not me,
 For I confound hell in elysium.

My ghost be with the old philosophers.
But leaving these vain trifles of men's souls,
Tell me, what is that Lucifer, thy lord?

MEPHOSTOPHILIS: Arch-regent and commander of all
spirits.

FAUSTUS: Was not that Lucifer an angel once?

MEPHOSTOPHILIS: Yes, Faustus, and most dearly loved of
God.

FAUSTUS: How comes it then that he is prince of devils?

MEPHOSTOPHILIS: Oh, by aspiring pride and insolence,
For which God threw him from the face of heaven.

FAUSTUS: And what are you that live with Lucifer?

MEPHOSTOPHILIS: Unhappy spirits that fell with Lucifer,
Conspired against our God with Lucifer,
And are for ever damned with Lucifer.

FAUSTUS: Where are you damned?

MEPHOSTOPHILIS: In hell.

FAUSTUS: How comes it then that thou art out of hell?

MEPHOSTOPHILIS: Why, this is hell, nor am I out of it.
Think'st thou that I that saw the face of God
And tasted the eternal joys of heaven,
Am not tormented with ten thousand hells
In being deprived of everlasting bliss?
Oh, Faustus, leave these frivolous demands,
Which strike a terror to my fainting soul.

FAUSTUS: What, is great Mephostophilis so passionate
For being deprived of the joys of heaven?
Learn thou of Faustus manly fortitude,
And scorn those joys thou never shalt possess.
Go, bear these tidings to great Lucifer,
Seeing Faustus hath incurred eternal death
By desperate thoughts against Jove's deity.
Say he surrenders up to him his soul,
So he will spare him four and twenty years,

Letting him live in all voluptuousness,
Having thee ever to attend on me,
To give me whatsoever I shall ask,
To tell me whatsoever I demand,
To slay mine enemies and to aid my friends
And always be obedient to my will.
Go, and return to mighty Lucifer,
And meet me in my study at midnight,
And then resolve me of thy master's mind.
MEPHOSTOPHILIS: I will, Faustus.
    Exit.

CHRISTOPHER MARLOWE,
Doctor Faustus, I, 3

To the Night

Swiftly walk over the western wave,
        Spirit of Night!
Out of the misty eastern cave
Where, all the long and lone daylight,
Thou wovest dreams of joy and fear
Which make thee terrible and dear, –
        Swift be thy flight!

Wrap thy form in a mantle gray
        Star-inwrought;
Blind with thine hair the eyes of Day,
Kiss her until she be wearied out:
Then wander o'er city and sea and land,
Touching all with thine opiate wand –
        Come, long-sought!

When I arose and saw the dawn,
   I sigh'd for thee;
When light rode high, and the dew was gone,
And noon lay heavy on flower and tree,
And the weary Day turn'd to his rest
Lingering like an unloved guest,
   I sigh'd for thee.

Thy brother Death came, and cried
   Wouldst thou me?
Thy sweet child Sleep, the filmy-eyed,
Murmur'd like a noon-tide bee
Shall I nestle near thy side?
Wouldst thou me? – And I replied
   No, not thee!

Death will come when thou art dead,
   Soon, too soon –
Sleep will come when thou art fled;
Of neither would I ask the boon
I ask of thee, belovèd Night –
Swift be thine approaching flight,
   Come soon, soon!

PERCY BYSSHE SHELLEY

The Retreat

Happy those early days! when I
Shined in my Angel-infancy.
Before I understood this place
Appointed for my second race,

Or taught my soul to fancy aught
But a white, celestial thought,
When yet I had not walked above
A mile, or two, from my first love,
And looking back (at that short space,)
Could see a glimpse of his bright face;
When on some *gilded cloud*, or *flower*
My gazing soul would dwell an hour,
And in those weaker glories spy
Some shadows of eternity;
Before I taught my tongue to wound
My conscience with a sinful sound,
Or had the black art to dispense
A several sin to every sense,
But felt through all this fleshly dress
Bright *shoots* of everlastingness.

    O how I long to travel back
And tread again that ancient track!
That I might once more reach that plain,
Where first I left my glorious train,
From whence the enlightened spirit sees
That shady city of palm trees;
But (ah!) my soul with too much stay
Is drunk, and staggers in the way.
Some men a forward motion love,
But I by backward steps would move,
And when this dust falls to the urn
In that state I came return.

HENRY VAUGHAN

Ode on Melancholy

No, no, go not to Lethe, neither twist
    Wolf's-bane, tight-rooted, for its poisonous wine:
Nor suffer thy pale forehead to be kissed
    By nightshade, ruby grape of Proserpine;
Make not your rosary of yew-berries,
    Nor let the beetle, nor the death-moth be
        Your mournful Psyche, nor the downy owl
A partner in your sorrow's mysteries;
    For shade to shade will come too drowsily,
        And drown the wakeful anguish of the soul.

But when the melancholy fit shall fall
    Sudden from heaven like a weeping cloud,
That fosters the droop-headed flowers all,
    And hides the green hill in an April shroud;
Then glut thy sorrow on a morning rose,
    Or on the rainbow of the salt sand-wave,
        Or on the wealth of globèd peonies;
Or if thy mistress some rich anger shows,
    Emprison her soft hand, and let her rave,
        And feed deep, deep upon her peerless eyes.

She dwells with Beauty – Beauty that must die;
    And Joy, whose hand is ever at his lips
Bidding adieu; and aching Pleasure nigh,
    Turning to poison while the bee-mouth sips:
Ay, in the very temple of Delight
    Veiled Melancholy has her sovran shrine,

Though seen of none save him whose strenuous tongue
  Can burst Joy's grape against his palate fine;
His soul shall taste the sadness of her might,
    And be among her cloudy trophies hung.

[Cancelled first stanza:]
Though you should build a bark of dead men's bones,
And rear a phantom gibbet for a mast,
Stitch creeds together for a sail, with groans
To fill it out, blood-stained and aghast;
Although your rudder be a dragon's tail
Long sever'd yet still hard with agony,
Your cordage large uprootings from the skull
Of bald Medusa, certes you would fail
To find the Melancholy – whether she
Dreameth in any isle of Lethe dull.

JOHN KEATS

Night Walks

Some years ago, a temporary inability to sleep, referable to a distressing impression, caused me to walk about the streets all night, for a series of several nights. The disorder might have taken a long time to conquer, if it had been faintly experimented on in bed; but, it was soon defeated by the brisk treatment of getting up directly after lying down, and going out, and coming home tired at sunrise.

In the course of those nights, I finished my education in a fair amateur experience of houselessness. My principal object being to get through the night, the pursuit of it brought me into sympathetic relations with people who have no other object every night in the year.

The month was March, and the weather damp, cloudy, and

cold. The sun not rising before half-past five, the night perspective looked sufficiently long at half-past twelve: which was about my time for confronting it.

The restlessness of a great city, and the way in which it tumbles and tosses before it can get to sleep, formed one of the first entertainments offered to the contemplation of us houseless people. It lasted about two hours. We lost a great deal of companionship when the late public-houses turned their lamps out, and when the potmen thrust the last brawling drunkards into the street; but stray vehicles and stray people were left us, after that. If we were very lucky, a policeman's rattle sprang and a fray turned up; but, in general, surprisingly little of this diversion was provided. Except in the Haymarket, which is the worst kept part of London, and about Kent-street in the Borough, and along a portion of the line of the Old Kent-road, the peace was seldom violently broken. But, it was always the case that London, as if in imitation of individual citizens belonging to it, had expiring fits and starts of restlessness. After all seemed quiet, if one cab rattled by, half-a-dozen would surely follow; and Houselessness even observed that intoxicated people appeared to be magnetically attracted towards each other: so that we knew when we saw one drunken object staggering against the shutters of a shop, that another drunken object would stagger up before five minutes were out, to fraternise or fight with it. When we made a divergence from the regular species of drunkard, the thin-armed, puff-faced, leaden-lipped gin-drinker, and encountered a rarer specimen of a more decent appearance, fifty to one but that specimen was dressed in soiled mourning. As the street experience in the night, so the street experience in the day; the common folk who come unexpectedly into a little property, come unexpectedly into a deal of liquor.

At length these flickering sparks would die away, worn out – the last veritable sparks of waking life trailed from some late pieman or hot-potato man – and London would sink to rest.

And then the yearning of the houseless mind would be for any sign of company, any lighted place, any movement, anything suggestive of any one being up – nay, even so much as awake, for the houseless eye looked out for lights in windows.

Walking the streets under the pattering rain, Houselessness would walk and walk and walk, seeing nothing but the interminable tangle of streets, save at a corner, here and there, two policemen in conversation, or the sergeant or inspector looking after his men. Now and then in the night – but rarely – Houselessness would become aware of a furtive head peering out of a doorway a few yards before him, and, coming up with the head, would find a man standing bolt upright to keep within the doorway's shadow, and evidently intent upon no particular service to society. Under a kind of fascination, and in a ghostly silence suitable to the time, Houselessness and this gentleman would eye one another from head to foot, and so, without exchange of speech, part, mutually suspicious. Drip, drip, drip, from ledge and coping, splash from pipes and water-spouts, and by-and-by the houseless shadow would fall upon the stones that pave the way to Waterloo-bridge; it being in the houseless mind to have a halfpenny worth of excuse for saying 'Good night' to the toll-keeper, and catching a glimpse of his fire. A good fire and a good great-coat and a good woollen neck-shawl, were comfortable things to see in conjunction with the toll-keeper; also his brisk wakefulness was excellent company when he rattled the change of halfpence down upon that metal table of his, like a man who defied the night, with all its sorrowful thoughts, and didn't care for the coming of dawn. There was need of encouragement on the threshold of the bridge, for the bridge was dreary. The chopped-up murdered man, had not been lowered with a rope over the parapet when those nights were; he was alive, and slept then quietly enough most likely, and undisturbed by any dream of where he was to come. But the river had an awful look, the buildings on the banks were muffled in black shrouds, and the reflected lights seemed to originate deep in the water, as if the spectres of suicides were holding them to show where they went down. The wild moon and clouds were as restless as an evil conscience in a tumbled bed, and the very shadow of the immensity of London seemed to lie oppressively upon the river.

Between the bridge and the two great theatres, there was but the distance of a few hundred paces, so the theatres came next. Grim and black within, at night, those great dry Wells, and lonesome to imagine, with the rows of faces faded out, the lights extinguished, and the seats all empty. One would think that nothing in them knew itself at such a time but Yorick's skull. In one of my night walks, as the church steeples were shaking the March winds and rain with strokes of Four, I passed the outer boundary of one of these great deserts, and entered it. With a dim lantern in my hand, I groped my well-known way to the stage and looked over the orchestra – which was like a great grave dug for a time of pestilence – into the void beyond. A dismal cavern of an immense aspect, with the chandelier gone dead like everything else, and nothing visible through mist and fog and space, but tiers of winding-sheets. The ground at my feet where, when last there, I had seen the peasantry of Naples dancing among the vines, reckless of the burning mountain which threatened to overwhelm them, was now in possession of a strong serpent of engine-hose, watchfully lying in wait for the serpent Fire, and ready to fly at it if it showed its forked tongue. A ghost of a watchman, carrying a faint corpse candle, haunted the distant upper gallery and flitted away. Retiring within the proscenium, and holding my light above my head towards the rolled-up curtain – green no more, but black as ebony – my sight lost itself in a gloomy vault, showing faint indications in it of a shipwreck of canvas and cordage. Methought I felt much as a diver might, at the bottom of the sea.

In those small hours when there was no movement in the

streets, it afforded matter for reflection to take Newgate in the way, and, touching its rough stone, to think of the prisoners in their sleep, and then to glance in at the lodge over the spiked wicket, and see the fire and light of the watching turnkeys, on the white wall. Not an inappropriate time either, to linger by that wicked little Debtors' Door – shutting tighter than any other door one ever saw – which has been Death's Door to so many. In the days of the uttering of forged one-pound notes by people tempted up from the country, how many hundreds of wretched creatures of both sexes – many quite innocent – swung out of a pitiless and inconsistent world, with the tower of yonder Christian church of Saint Sepulchre monstrously before their eyes! Is there any haunting of the Bank Parlour, by the remorseful souls of old directors, in the nights of these later days, I wonder, or is it as quiet as this degenerate Aceldama of an Old Bailey?

To walk on the Bank, lamenting the good old times and bemoaning the present evil period, would be an easy next step, so I would take it, and would make my houseless circuit of the Bank, and give a thought to the treasure within; likewise to the guard of soldiers passing the night there, and nodding over the fire. Next, I went to Billingsgate, in some hope of market-people, but it proving as yet too early, crossed London-bridge and got down by the waterside on the Surrey shore among the buildings of the great brewery. There was plenty going on at the brewery; and the reek, and the smell of grains, and the rattling of the plump dray horses at their mangers, were capital company. Quite refreshed by having mingled with this good society, I made a new start with a new heart, setting the old King's Bench prison before me for my next object, and resolving, when I should come to the wall, to think of poor Horace Kinch, and the Dry Rot in men.

A very curious disease the Dry Rot in men, and difficult to detect the beginning of. It had carried Horace Kinch inside the wall of the old King's Bench prison, and it had carried him out with his feet foremost. He was a likely man to look at, in the prime of life, well to do, as clever as he needed to be, and popular among many friends. He was suitably married, and had healthy and pretty children. But, like some fair-looking houses or fair-looking ships, he took the Dry Rot. The first strong external revelation of the Dry Rot in men, is a tendency to lurk and lounge; to be at street-corners without intelligible reason; to be going anywhere when met; to be about many places rather than at any; to do nothing tangible, but to have an intention of performing a variety of intangible duties to-morrow or the day after. When this manifestation of the disease is observed, the observer will usually connect it with a vague impression once formed or received, that the patient was living a little too hard. He will scarcely have had leisure to turn it over in his mind and form the terrible suspicion 'Dry Rot,' when he will notice a change for the worse in the patient's appearance: a certain slovenliness and deterioration, which is not poverty, nor dirt, nor intoxication, nor ill-health, but simply Dry Rot. To this, succeeds a smell as of strong waters, in the morning; to that, a looseness respecting money; to that, a stronger smell as of strong waters, at all times; to that, a looseness respecting everything; to that, a trembling of the limbs, somnolency, misery, and crumbling to pieces. As it is in wood, so it is in men. Dry rot advances at a compound usury quite incalculable. A plank is found infected with it, and the whole structure is devoted. Thus it had been with the unhappy Horace Kinch, lately buried by a small subscription. Those who knew him had not nigh done saying, 'So well off, so comfortably established, with such hope before him – and yet, it is feared, with a slight touch of Dry Rot!' when lo! the man was all Dry Rot and dust.

From the dead wall associated on those houseless nights with this too common story, I chose next to wander by Bethlehem Hospital; partly, because it lay on my road round to Westminster; partly, because I had a night fancy in my head which could be best pursued within sight of its walls and dome. And the fancy was this: Are not the sane and the insane equal at night as the sane lie a dreaming? Are not all of us outside this hospital, who dream, more or less in the condition of those inside it, every night of our lives? Are we not nightly persuaded, as they daily are, that we associate preposterously with kings and queens, emperors and empresses, and notabilities of all sorts? Do we not nightly jumble events and personages and times and places, as these do daily? Are we not sometimes troubled by our own sleeping inconsistencies, and do we not vexedly try to account for them or excuse them, just as these do sometimes in respect of their waking delusions? Said an afflicted man to me, when I was last in a hospital like this, 'Sir, I can frequently fly.' I was half ashamed to reflect that so could I – by night. Said a woman to me on the same occasion, 'Queen Victoria frequently comes to dine with me, and her Majesty and I dine off peaches and maccaroni in our night-gowns, and his Royal Highness the Prince Consort does us the honour to make a third on horseback in a Field-Marshal's uniform.' Could I refrain from reddening with consciousness when I remembered the amazing royal parties I myself had given (at night), the unaccountable viands I had put on table, and my extraordinary manner of conducting myself on those distinguished occasions? I wonder that the great master who knew everything, when he called Sleep the death of each day's life, did not call Dreams the insanity of each day's sanity.

By this time I had left the Hospital behind me, and was again setting towards the river; and in a short breathing space I was on Westminster-bridge, regaling my houseless eyes with the external walls of the British Parliament – the perfection of a stupendous institution, I know, and the admiration of all surrounding nations and succeeding ages, I do not doubt, but perhaps a little the better now and then for being pricked up to its work. Turning off into Old Palace-yard, the Courts of Law kept me company for a quarter of an hour; hinting in low whispers what numbers of people they were keeping awake, and how intensely wretched and horrible they were rendering the small hours to unfortunate suitors. Westminster Abbey was fine gloomy society for another quarter of an hour; suggesting a wonderful procession of its dead among the dark arches and pillars, each century more amazed by the century following it than by all the centuries going before. And indeed in those houseless night walks – which even included cemeteries where watchmen went round among the graves at stated times, and moved the tell-tale handle of an index which recorded that they had touched it at such an hour – it was a solemn consideration what enormous hosts of dead belong to one old great city, and how, if they were raised while the living slept, there would not be the space of a pin's point in all the streets and ways for the living to come out into. Not only that, but the vast armies of dead would overflow the hills and valleys beyond the city, and would stretch away all round it, God knows how far.

When a church clock strikes, on houseless ears in the dead of night, it may be at first mistaken for company and hailed as such. But, as the spreading circles of vibration, which you may perceive at such a time with great clearness, go opening out, for ever and ever afterwards widening perhaps (as the philosopher has suggested) in eternal space, the mistake is rectified and the sense of loneliness is profounder. Once – it was after leaving the Abbey and turning my face north – I came to the great steps of St. Martin's church as the clock was striking Three. Suddenly, a thing that in a moment more I should have trodden upon without seeing, rose up at my feet with a cry of loneliness and houselessness, struck out of it by the bell, the like of which I never heard. We then stood face to face looking at one another, frightened by one another. The creature was like a beetle-browed hair-lipped youth of twenty, and it had a loose bundle of rags on, which it held together with one of its hands. It shivered from head to foot, and its teeth chattered, and as it stared at me – persecutor, devil, ghost, whatever it thought me – it made with its whining mouth as if it were snapping at me, like a worried dog. Intending to give this ugly object money, I put my hand to stay it – for it recoiled as it whined and snapped – and laid my hand upon its shoulder. Instantly, it twisted out of its garment, like the young man in the New Testament, and left me standing alone with its rags in my hands.

Covent-garden Market, when it was market morning, was wonderful company. The great waggons of cabbages, with growers' men and boys lying asleep under them, and with sharp dogs from market-garden neighbourhoods looking after the whole, were as good as a party. But one of the worst night sights I know in London, is to be found in the children who prowl about this place; who sleep in the baskets, fight for the offal, dart at any object they think they can lay their thieving hands on, dive under the carts and barrows, dodge the constables, and are perpetually making a blunt pattering on the pavement of the Piazza with the rain of their naked feet. A painful and unnatural result comes of the comparison one is forced to institute between the growth of corruption as displayed in the so much improved and cared for fruits of the earth, and the growth of corruption as displayed in these all uncared for (except inasmuch as ever-hunted) savages.

There was early coffee to be got about Covent-garden Market, and that was more company – warm company, too, which was better. Toast of a very substantial quality, was likewise procurable: though the towzled-headed man who made it, in an inner chamber within the coffee-room, hadn't got his coat on yet, and was so heavy with sleep that in every interval of toast and coffee he went off anew behind the partition into complicated cross-roads of choke and snore, and lost his way directly. Into one of these establishments (among the earliest) near Bow-street, there came one morning as I sat over my houseless cup, pondering where to go next, a man in a high and long snuff-coloured coat, and shoes, and, to the best of my belief, nothing else but a hat, who took out of his hat a large cold meat pudding; a meat pudding so large that it was a very tight fit, and brought the lining of the hat out with it. This mysterious man was known by his pudding, for on his entering, the man of sleep brought him a pint of hot tea, a small loaf, and a large knife and fork and plate. Left to himself in his box, he stood the pudding on the bare table, and, instead of cutting it, stabbed it, overhand, with the knife, like a mortal enemy; then took the knife out, wiped it on his sleeve, tore the pudding asunder with his fingers, and ate it all up. The remembrance of this man with the pudding remains with me as the remembrance of the most spectral person my houselessness encountered. Twice only was I in that establishment, and twice I saw him stalk in (as I should say, just out of bed, and presently going back to bed), take out his pudding, stab his pudding, wipe the dagger, and eat his pudding all up. He was a man whose figure promised cadaverousness, but who had an excessively red face, though shaped like a horse's. On the second occasion of my seeing him, he said huskily to the man of sleep, 'Am I red to-night?' 'You are,' he uncompromisingly answered. 'My mother,' said the spectre, 'was a red-faced woman that liked drink, and I looked at her hard when she laid in her coffin, and I took the complexion.' Somehow, the pudding seemed an unwholesome pudding after that, and I put myself in its way no more.

When there was no market, or when I wanted variety, a railway terminus with the morning mails coming in, was remunerative company. But like most of the company to be had in this world, it lasted only a very short time. The station lamps would burst out ablaze, the porters would emerge from places of conceal-ment, the cabs and trucks would rattle to their places (the post-office carts were already in theirs), and, finally, the bell would strike up, and the train would come banging in. But there were few passengers and little luggage, and everything scuttled away with the greatest expedition. The locomotive post-offices, with their great nets – as if they had been dragging the country for bodies – would fly open as to their doors, and would disgorge a smell of lamp, an exhausted clerk, a guard in a red coat, and their bags of letters; the engine would blow and heave and perspire, like an engine wiping its forehead and saying what a run it had had; and within ten minutes the lamps were out, and I was houseless and alone again.

But now, there were driven cattle on the high road near, wanting (as cattle always do) to turn into the midst of stone walls, and squeeze themselves through six inches' width of iron railing, and getting their heads down (also as cattle always do) for tossing-purchase at quite imaginary dogs, and giving themselves and every devoted creature associated with them a most extraordinary amount of unnecessary trouble. Now, too, the conscious gas began to grow pale with the knowledge that daylight was coming, and straggling work-people were already in the streets, and, as waking life had become extinguished with the last pieman's sparks, so it began to be rekindled with the fires of the first street-corner breakfast-sellers. And so by faster and faster degrees, until the last degrees were very fast, the day came, and I was tired and could sleep. And it is not, as I used to think, going home at such times, the least wonderful thing in London, that in the real desert region of the night, the houseless wanderer is alone there. I knew well enough where to find Vice and Misfortune of all kinds, if I had chosen; but they were put out of sight, and my houselessness had many miles upon miles of streets in which it could, and did, have its own solitary way.

CHARLES DICKENS

Psalm 102

Lord, hear my pray'r, and let my cry pass
    Unto the Lord without impediment.
    Do not from me turn thy merciful face,
Unto myself leaving my government.
    In time of trouble and adversity
    Incline to me thine ear and thine intent;
And when I call, help my necessity:
    Readily grant th' effect of my desire.
    These bold demands do please thy majesty,
And eke my case such haste doth well require.
    For like as smoke my days been passed away,
    My bones dried up as furnace with the fire,
My heart, my mind is withered up like hay
    Because I have forgot to take my bread,
    My bread of life, the word of truth, I say:
And for my plaintful sighès, and my dread,
    My bones, my strength, my very force of mind
    Cleaved to the flesh and from the sprite were fled,
As desperate thy mercy for to find.
    So made I me the solaine pelican,
    And like the owl that fleeth by proper kind
Light of the day and hath her self beta'en
    To ruin life out of all company.
    With waker care that with this woe began,
Like the sparrow was I solitary,
    That sits alone under the house's eaves.
    This while my foes conspired continually,
And did provoke the harm of my disease
    Wherefore like ashes my bread did me savour,
    Of thy just word the taste might not me please.

Wherefore my drink I tempered with liqueur
   Of weeping tears that from mine eyes do rain:
   Because I know the wrath of thy furor
Provok'd by right had of my pride disdain;
   For thou didst lift me up to throw me down,
   To teach me how to know my self again.
Whereby I know that helpless I should drown,
   My days like shadow decline and I do dry;
   And thee forever eternity doth crown;
World without end doth last thy memory.
   For this frailtee that yoketh all mankind,
   Thou shalt awake and rue this misery,
Rue on Zion, Zion that as I find
   Is the people that live under thy law;
   For now is time, the time at hand assign'd,
The time so long that doth thy servants draw
   In great desire to see that pleasant day,
   Day of redeeming Zion from sin's awe:
For they have ruth to see in such decay
   In dust and stones this wretched Zion low'r.
   Then the gentiles shall dread thy name alway;
All earthly kings thy glory shall honour,
   Then when that grace thy Zion thus redeemeth,
   When thus thou hast declar'd thy mighty pow'r.
The Lord his servants' wishes so esteemeth
   That he him turneth unto the poors' request.
   To our descent this to be written seemeth,
Of all comforts as consolation best;
   And they that then shall be regenerate
   Shall praise the Lord therefore both most and least.
For he hath look'd from the height of his estate,
   The Lord from heaven in earth hath looked on us,
   To hear the moan of them that are algate

In foul bondage: to loose and to discuss
   The sons of death from out their deadly bond,
   To give thereby occasion gracious
In this Zion his holy name to stand
   And in Jerusalem his laudès lasting aye:
   When in one church the people of the land
And realms been gather'd to serve to laud, to pray
   The Lord alone so just and merciful.
   But to this assembly running in the way
My strength faileth to reach it at the full.
   He hath abridg'd my days; they may not dure,
   To see that term, that term so wonderful.
Although I have with hearty will and Cure
   Prayed to the Lord: 'Take me not, Lord, away
   In middès of my years, though thine ever sure
Remain eterne, whom time can not decay.
   Thou wrought'st the earth, thy hands th' heavens did make;
   They shall perish and thou shalt last alway,
And all things Age shall wear and overtake
   Like cloth; and thou shalt change them like apparel,
   Turn and translate and they in worth it take.
But thou thy self the self remainest well
   That thou wast erst, and shall thy years extend.
   Then since to this there may no thing rebel,
The greatest comfort that I can pretend
   Is that the children of thy servants dear
   That in thy word are got shall without end
Before thy face be stablish'd all in fear.'

SIR THOMAS WYATT

Psalm 102

1. Hear my prayer, O Lord: and let my crying come unto thee.

2. Hide not thy face from me in the time of my trouble: incline thine ear unto me when I call; O hear me, and that right soon.

3. For my days are consumed away like smoke: and my bones are burnt up as it were a fire-brand.

4. My heart is smitten down, and withered like grass: so that I forget to eat my bread.

5. For the voice of my groaning: my bones will scarce cleave to my flesh.

6. I am become like a pelican in the wilderness: and like an owl that is in the desert.

7. I have watched, and am even as it were a sparrow: that sitteth alone upon the house-top.

8. Mine enemies revile me all the day long: and they that are mad upon me are sworn together against me.

9. For I have eaten ashes as it were bread: and mingled my drink with weeping;

10. And that because of thine indignation and wrath: for thou hast taken me up, and cast me down.

11. My days are gone like a shadow: and I am withered like grass.

12. But thou, O Lord, shalt endure for ever: and thy remembrance throughout all generations.

13. Thou shalt arise, and have mercy upon Sion: for it is time that thou have mercy upon her, yea, the time is come.

14. And why? thy servants think upon her stones: and it pitieth them to see her in the dust.

15. The heathen shall fear thy Name, O Lord: and all the kings of the earth thy Majesty;

16. When the Lord shall build up Sion: and when his glory shall appear;

17. When he turneth him unto the prayer of the poor destitute: and despiseth not their desire.

18. This shall be written for those that come after: and the people which shall be born shall praise the Lord.

19. For he hath looked down from his sanctuary: out of the heaven did the Lord behold the earth;

20. That he might hear the mournings of such as are in captivity: and deliver the children appointed unto death;

21. That they may declare the Name of the Lord in Sion: and his worship at Jerusalem;

22. When the people are gathered together: and the kingdoms also, to serve the Lord.

23. He brought down my strength in my journey: and shortened my days.

24. But I said, O my God, take me not away in the midst of mine age: as for thy years, they endure throughout all generations.

25. Thou, Lord, in the beginning hast laid the foundation of the earth: and the heavens are the work of thy hands.

26. They shall perish, but thou shalt endure: they all shall wax old as doth a garment;

27. And as a vesture shalt thou change them, and they shall be changed: but thou art the same, and thy years shall not fail.

28. The children of thy servants shall continue: and their seed shall stand fast in thy sight.

MILES COVERDALE

from *Psalm 102*

When I pour out my Soul in Pray'r,
    Do thou, O Lord, attend:
To thy Eternal Throne of Grace
    Let my sad Cry ascend.

O hide not thou thy glorious Face
    In times of deep Distress,
Incline thine Ear, and when I call
    My Sorrows soon redress.

Each cloudy Portion of my Life
    Like scatter'd Smoke expires;
My shriv'led Bones are like a Hearth
    That's parch'd with constant Fires.

My Heart, like Grass that feels the Blast
    Of some infectious Wind,
Is wither'd so with Grief, that scarce
    My needful Food I mind.

By reason of my sad Estate
    I spend my Breath in Groans;
My Flesh is worn away, my Skin
    Scarce hides my starting Bones.

I'm like a Pelican become,
    That does in Deserts mourn;
Or like an Owl that sits all day
    On barren Trees forlorn.

In Watchings or in restless Dreams
   I spend the tedious Night;
Like Sparrows, that on Houses' tops
   To sit alone delight.

All day by railing Foes I'm made
   The Object of their Scorn;
Who all, inspir'd with furious Rage,
   Have my Destruction sworn.

In dust I lie, and all my Bread
   With ashes mixed appears;
When e'er I quench my burning Thirst,
   My Drink is dash'd with Tears.

Because on me with Double weight
   Thy heavy Wrath does lie;
For thou to make my Fall more great
   Didst lift me up on high.

My Days are like the Ev'ning Shade
   That hastily declines.
My Beauty too, like wither'd Grass,
   With faded Lustre pines:

But thy eternal State, O Lord,
   No length of Time shall waste,
The mem'ry of thy wond'rous Works
   From Age to Age shall last.

NAHUM TATE AND NICHOLAS BRADY

from *Psalm 102*

It is the Lord our Saviour's hand,
Weakens our strength amidst the race.
Disease and death, at his command,
Arrest us, and cut short our days.

Spare us, O Lord, aloud we pray,
Nor let our sun go down at noon:
Thy years are one eternal day,
And must thy children die so soon!

Yet, in the midst of death and grief,
This thought our sorrow shall assuage:
'Our Father and our Saviour live;
Christ is the same through ev'ry age'.

'Twas He this earth's foundation laid;
Heaven is the building of his hand:
This earth grows old, these heavens shall fade,
And all be chang'd at his command.

The starry curtains of the sky,
Like garments, shall be laid aside;
But still thy throne stands firm and high;
Thy church for ever must abide.

Before thy face thy church shall live,
And on thy throne thy children reign:
This dying world shall they survive,
And the dead saints be rais'd again.

ISAAC WATTS

Psalm 102

Lord, hear my prayer when trouble glooms,
Let sorrow find a way,
And when the day of trouble comes,
Turn not thy face away:
My bones like hearthstones burn away,
My life like vapoury smoke decays.

My heart is smitten like the grass,
That withered lies and dead,
And I, so lost to what I was,
Forget to eat my bread.
My voice is groaning all the day,
My bones prick through this skin of clay.

The wilderness's pelican,
The desert's lonely owl –
I am their like, a desert man
In ways as lone and foul.
As sparrows on the cottage top
I wait till I with fainting drop.

I hear my enemies reproach,
All silently I mourn;
They on my private peace encroach,
Against me they are sworn.
Ashes as bread my trouble shares,
And mix my food with weeping cares.

Yet not for them is sorrow's toil,
I fear no mortal's frowns –
But thou hast held me up awhile

And thou hast cast me down.
My days like shadows waste from view,
I mourn like withered grass in dew.

But thou, Lord, shalt endure for ever,
All generations through;
Thou shalt to Zion be the giver
Of joy and mercy too.
Her very stones are in thy trust,
Thy servants reverence her dust.

Heathens shall hear and fear thy name,
All kings on earth thy glory know
When thou shalt build up Zion's fame
And live in glory there below.
He'll not despise their prayers, though mute,
But still regard the destitute.

JOHN CLARE

Ghosts

Horror ubique animos, simul ipsa silentia terrent. Virgil

At a little Distance from Sir ROGER's House, among the Ruins
of an old Abbey, there is a long Walk of aged Elms; which are
shot up so very high, that when one passes under them, the
Rooks and Crows that rest upon the Tops of them seem to be
Cawing in another Region. I am very much delighted with this
Sort of Noise, which I consider as a kind of natural Prayer to
that Being who supplies the Wants of his whole Creation, and,
who in the beautiful Language of the *Psalms*, feedeth the young
Ravens that call upon him. I like this Retirement the better,

because of an ill Report it lies under of being *haunted*; for which Reason (as I have been told in the Family) no living Creature ever walks in it besides the Chaplain. My good Friend the Butler desired me with a very grave Face not to venture myself in it after Sun-set, for that one of the Footmen had been almost frighted out of his Wits by a Spirit that appeared to him in the Shape of a black Horse without an Head; to which he added, that about a Month ago one of the Maids coming home late that Way with a Pail of Milk upon her Head, heard such a Rustling among the Bushes that she let it fall.

I was taking a Walk in this Place last Night between the Hours of Nine and Ten, and could not but fancy it one of the most proper Scenes in the World for a Ghost to appear in. The Ruins of the Abby are scattered up and down on every Side, and half covered with Ivy and Elder-Bushes, the Harbours of several solitary Birds which seldom make their Appearance till the Dusk of the Evening. The Place was formerly a Church-yard, and has still several Marks in it of Graves and Burying-Places. There is such an Eccho among the old Ruins and Vaults, that if you stamp but a little louder than ordinary you hear the Sound repeated. At the same Time the Walk of Elms, with the Croaking of the Ravens which from time to time are heard from the Tops of them, looks exceeding solemn and venerable. These Objects naturally raise Seriousness and Attention; and when Night heightens the Awfulness of the Place, and pours out her supernumerary Horrours upon every thing in it, I do not at all wonder that weak Minds fill it with Spectres and Apparitions.

Mr. *Locke*, in his Chapter of the Association of Ideas, has very curious Remarks to shew how by the Prejudice of Education one Idea often introduces into the Mind a whole Set that bear no Resemblance to one another in the Nature of things. Among several Examples of this Kind, he produces the following Instance. *The Ideas of Goblins and Sprights have really no more to do with Darkness than Light: Yet let but a foolish Maid inculcate these often on the Mind of a Child, and raise them there together, possibly he shall never bee able to separate them again so long as he lives; but Darkness shall ever afterwards bring with it those frightful Ideas, and they shall be so joyned, that he can no more bear the one than the other.*

As I was walking in this Solitude, where the Dusk of the Evening conspired with so many other Occasions of Terrour, I observed a Cow grazing not far from me, which an Imagination that is apt to *startle* might easily have construed into a black Horse without an Head; and I dare say the poor Footman lost his Wits upon some such trivial Occasion.

My friend Sir ROGER has often told me with a great deal of Mirth, that at first coming to his Estate he found three Parts of his House altogether useless; that the best Room in it had the Reputation of being haunted, and by that Means was locked up; that Noises had been heard in his long Gallery, so that he could not get a Servant to enter it after eight a Clock at Night; that the Door of one of his Chambers was nailed up, because there went a Story in the Family that a Butler had formerly hanged himself in it; and that his Mother, who lived to a great Age, had shut up half the Rooms in the House, in which either her Husband, a Son, or Daughter had died. The Knight seeing his Habitation reduced to so small a Compass and himself in a Manner shut out of his own House, upon the Death of his Mother ordered all the Apartments to be flung open, and *exorcised* by his Chaplain, who lay in every Room one after another, and by that Means dissipated the Fears which had so long reigned in the Family.

I should not have been thus particular upon these ridiculous Horrours, did not I find them so very much prevail in all Parts of the Country. At the same Time I think a Person who is thus terrifyed with the Imagination of Ghosts and Spectres much more reasonable, than one who contrary to the Reports of all Historians sacred and prophane, ancient and modern, and to the Traditions of all Nations, thinks the Appearance of Spirits fabulous and groundless; Could not I give my self up to this general Testimony of Mankind, I should to the Relations of particular Persons who are now living, and whom I cannot distrust in other Matters of Fact, I might here add, that not only the Historians, to whom we may joyn the Poets, but likewise the Philosophers of Antiquity have favoured this Opinion. *Lucretius* himself, though by the Course of his Philosophy he was obliged to maintain that the Soul did not exist separate from the Body, makes no Doubt of the Reality of Apparitions, and that Men have often appeared after their Death. This I think very remarkable; he was so pressed with the Matter of Fact which he could not have the Confidence to deny, that he was forced to account for it by one of the most absurd unphilosophical Notions that was ever started. He tells us, That the Surfaces of all Bodies are perpetually flying off from their respective Bodies, one after another; and that these Surfaces or thin Cases that included each other whilst they were joined in the Body like the Coats of an Onion, are sometimes seen entire when they are separated from it; by which Means we often behold the Shapes and Shadows of Persons who are either dead or absent.

I shall dismiss this Paper with a Story out of *Josephus*, not so much for the Sake of the Story it self, as for the moral Reflections with which the Author concludes it, and which I shall here set down in his own Words. '*Glaphyra* the Daughter of King *Archilaus*, after the Death of her two first Husbands (being married to a third, who was Brother to her first Husband, and so passionately in Love with her that he turned off his former Wife to make Room for this Marriage) had a very odd kind of Dream. She fancied that she saw her first Husband coming towards her, and that she embraced him with great Tenderness; when in the Midst of the Pleasure which she expressed at the Sight of him, he reproached her after the following Manner: *Glaphyra*, says he, thou hast made good the old Saying, That

Women are not to be trusted. Was not I the Husband of thy Virginity? have I not Children by thee? How couldst thou forget our Loves so far as to enter into a second Marriage, and after that into a third, nay to take for thy Husband a Man who has so shamele[s]sly crept into the Bed of his Brother? However, for the Sake of our passed Loves, I shall free thee from thy present Reproach, and make thee mine for ever. *Glaphyra* told this Dream to several Women of her Acquaintance, and died soon after. I thought this Story might not be impertinent in this Place, wherein I speak of those Things: Besides that, the Example deserves to be taken Notice of, as it contains a most certain Proof of the Immortality of the Soul, and of Divine Providence. If any Man thinks these Facts incredible, let him enjoy his Opinion to himself; but let him not endeavour to disturb the Belief of others, who by Instances of this Nature are excited to the Study of Virtue.'

JOSEPH ADDISON,
from *The Spectator*, No. 110

The Darkling Thrush

The land's sharp features seemed to be
   The Century's corpse outleant,
His crypt the cloudy canopy,
   The wind his death-lament.
The ancient pulse of germ and birth
   Was shrunken hard and dry,
And every spirit upon earth
   Seemed fervourless as I.

At once a voice arose among
    The bleak twigs overhead
In a full-hearted evensong
    Of joy illimited;
An aged thrush, frail, gaunt, and small,
    In blast-beruffled plume,
Had chosen thus to fling his soul
    Upon the growing gloom.

So little cause for carolings
    Of such ecstatic sound
Was written on terrestrial things
    Afar or nigh around,
That I could think there trembled through
    His happy good-night air
Some blessed Hope, whereof he knew
    And I was unaware.

I leant upon a coppice gate
    When Frost was spectre-gray,
And Winter's dregs made desolate
    The weakening eye of day.
The tangled bine-stems scored the sky
    Like strings of broken lyres,
And all mankind that haunted nigh
    Had sought their household fires.

THOMAS HARDY

Melancholy

None of these spirits of the air or the fire have so much predominance in the night as the spirits of the earth and the water; for they feeding on foggy-brained melancholy engender thereof many uncouth terrible monsters. Thus much observe by the way, that the grossest part of our blood is the melancholy humour, which in the spleen congealed whose office is to disperse it, with his thick steaming fenny vapours casteth a mist over the spirit and clean bemasketh the fantasy.

And even as slime and dirt in a standing puddle engender toads and frogs and many other unsightly creatures, so this slimy melancholy humour, still still thickening as it stands still, engendreth many misshapen objects in our imaginations. Sundry times we behold whole armies of men skirmishing in the air: dragons, wild beasts, bloody streamers, blazing comets, fiery streaks, with other apparitions innumerable. Whence have all these their conglomerate matter but from fuming meteors that arise from the earth? So from the fuming melancholy of our spleen mounteth that hot matter into the higher region of the brain, whereof many fearful visions are framed. Our reason even like drunken fumes it displaceth and intoxicates, and yields up our intellective apprehension to be mocked and trodden under foot by every false object or counterfeit noise that comes near it. Herein specially consisteth our senses' defect and abuse, that those organical parts, which to the mind are ordained ambassadors, do not their message as they ought, but, by some misdiet or misgovernment being distempered, fail in their report and deliver up nothing but lies and fables.

Such is our brain oppressed with melancholy, as is a clock tied down with too heavy weights or plummets; which as it cannot choose but monstrously go a-square or not go at all, so

must our brains of necessity be either monstrously distracted
or utterly destroyed thereby.

THOMAS NASHE,
from *The Terrors of the Night or*
A Discourse of Apparitions

Frost at Midnight

The frost performs its secret ministry,
Unhelped by any wind. The owlet's cry
Came loud – and hark, again! loud as before.
The inmates of my cottage, all at rest,
Have left me to that solitude, which suits
Abstruser musings: save that at my side
My cradled infant slumbers peacefully.
'Tis calm indeed! so calm, that it disturbs
And vexes meditation with its strange
And extreme silentness. Sea, hill, and wood,
This populous village! Sea, and hill, and wood,
With all the numberless goings on of life,
Inaudible as dreams! the thin blue flame
Lies on my low burnt fire, and quivers not;
Only that film, which fluttered on the grate,
Still flutters there, the sole unquiet thing.
Methinks, its motion in this hush of nature
Gives it dim sympathies with me who live,
Making it a companionable form,
Whose puny flaps and freaks the idling Spirit
By its own moods interprets, every where
Echo or mirror seeking of itself,
And makes a toy of Thought.

                        But O! how oft,
How oft, at school, with most believing mind,

Presageful, have I gazed upon the bars,
To watch that fluttering stranger! and as oft
With unclosed lids, already had I dreamt
Of my sweet birth-place, and the old church-tower,
Whose bells, the poor man's only music, rang
From morn to evening, all the hot Fair-day,
So sweetly, that they stirred and haunted me
With a wild pleasure, falling on mine ear
Most like articulate sounds of things to come!
So gazed I, till the soothing things I dreamt
Lulled me to sleep, and sleep prolonged my dreams!
And so I brooded all the following morn,
Awed by the stern preceptor's face, mine eye
Fixed with mock study on my swimming book:
Save if the door half opened, and I snatched
A hasty glance, and still my heart leaped up,
For still I hoped to see the stranger's face,
Townsman, or aunt, or sister more beloved,
My play-mate when we both were clothed alike!

Dear Babe, that sleepest cradled by my side,
Whose gentle breathings, heard in this deep calm,
Fill up the interspersed vacancies
And momentary pauses of the thought!
My babe so beautiful! it thrills my heart
With tender gladness, thus to look at thee,
And think that thou shalt learn far other lore
And in far other scenes! For I was reared
In the great city, pent 'mid cloisters dim,
And saw nought lovely but the sky and stars.
But thou, my babe! shalt wander like a breeze
By lakes and sandy shores, beneath the crags
Of ancient mountain, and beneath the clouds,
Which image in their bulk both lakes and shores

And mountain crags: so shalt thou see and hear
The lovely shapes and sounds intelligible
Of that eternal language, which thy God
Utters, who from eternity doth teach
Himself in all, and all things in himself.
Great universal Teacher! he shall mould
Thy spirit, and by giving make it ask.

Therefore all seasons shall be sweet to thee,
Whether the summer clothe the general earth
With greenness, or the redbreast sit and sing
Betwixt the tufts of snow on the bare branch
Of mossy apple-tree, while the nigh thatch
Smokes in the sun-thaw; whether the eve-drops fall
Heard only in the trances of the blast,
Or if the secret ministry of frost
Shall hang them up in silent icicles,
Quietly shining to the quiet Moon.

SAMUEL TAYLOR COLERIDGE

'The night is darkening round me'

The night is darkening round me
The wild winds coldly blow
But a tyrant spell has bound me
And I cannot cannot go

The giant trees are bending
Their bare boughs weighed with snow
And the storm is fast descending
And yet I cannot go

Clouds beyond clouds above me
Wastes beyond wastes below
But nothing drear can move me
I will not cannot go

EMILY BRONTË

The Valley of the Shadow of Death

Now at the end of this Valley, was another, called the Valley of the Shadow of Death, and Christian must needs go through it because the way to the Celestial City lay through the midst of it: now this Valley is a very solitary place. The prophet Jeremiah thus describes it, *A wilderness, a land of deserts, and of pits, a land of drought, and of the shadow of death, a land that no man* (but a Christian) *passeth through, and where no man dwelt.*

Now here Christian was worse put to it than in his fight with Apollyon, as by the sequel you shall see.

I saw then in my dream, that when Christian was got to the borders of the Shadow of Death there met him two men, children of them that brought up an evil report of the good land, making haste to go back: to whom Christian spake as follows.

Christian. Whither are you going?

Men. They said, Back, back; and would have you to do so too, if either life or peace is prized by you.

Christian. Why? what's the matter? said Christian.

Men. Matter! said they; we were going that way as you are going, and went as far as we durst; and indeed we were almost past coming back, for had we gone a little further, we had not been here to bring the news to thee.

Christian. But what have you met with? said Christian.

Men. Why we were almost in the Valley of the Shadow of

Death, but that by good hap we looked before us, and saw the danger before we came to it.

Christian. But what have you seen? said Christian.

Men. Seen! Why the Valley itself, which is as dark as pitch; we also saw there the hobgoblins, satyrs, and dragons of the pit: we heard also in that Valley a continual howling and yelling, as of a people under unutterable misery who there sat bound in affliction and irons: and over that Valley hangs the discouraging clouds of confusion; death also doth always spread his wings over it: in a word, it is every whit dreadful, being utterly without order.

Christian. Then said Christian, I perceive not yet, by what you have said, but that this is my way to the desired haven.

Men. Be it thy way, we will not choose it for ours. So they parted, and Christian went on his way, but still with his sword drawn in his hand, for fear lest he should be assaulted.

I saw then in my dream so far as this Valley reached, there was on the right hand a very deep ditch, that ditch is it into which the blind have led the blind in all ages, and have both there miserably perished. Again, behold on the left hand there was a very dangerous quag, into which, if even a good man falls he can find no bottom for his foot to stand on. Into that quag King David once did fall, and had no doubt therein been smothered, had not he that is able plucked him out.

The pathway was here also exceeding narrow, and therefore good Christian was the more put to it; for when he sought in the dark to shun the ditch on the one hand, he was ready to tip over into the mire on the other; also when he sought to escape the mire, without great carefulness he would be ready to fall into the ditch. Thus he went on, and I heard him here sigh bitterly, for, besides the dangers mentioned above, the pathway was here so dark that oft times when he lift up his foot to set forward he knew not where, or upon what, he should set it next.

About the midst of this Valley, I perceived the mouth of Hell to be, and it stood also hard by the wayside. Now, thought Christian, what shall I do? And ever and anon the flame and smoke would come out in such abundance, with sparks and hideous noises (things that cared not for Christian's sword, as did Apollyon before) that he was forced to put up his sword, and betake himself to another weapon called All-Prayer: so he cried in my hearing, '*O Lord I beseech thee deliver my Soul.*' Thus he went on a great while, yet still the flames would be reaching towards him: also he heard doleful voices, and rushings too and fro, so that sometimes he thought he should be torn to pieces, or trodden down like mire in the streets. This frightful sight was seen, and these dreadful noises were heard by him, for several miles together: and coming to a place where he thought he heard a company of fiends coming forward to meet him, he stopped, and began to muse what he had best to do. Sometimes he had half a thought to go back. Then again he thought he might be halfway through the Valley; he remembered also how he had already vanquished many a danger: and that the danger of going back might be much more than for to go forward; so he resolved to go on. Yet the fiends seemed to come nearer and nearer, but when they were come even almost at him, he cried out with a most vehement voice, 'I will walk in the strength of the Lord God'; so they gave back, and came no further.

One thing I would not let slip, I took notice that now poor Christian was so confounded that he did not know his own voice, and thus I perceived it: just when he was come over against the mouth of the burning pit, one of the wicked ones got behind him, and stepped up softly to him, and whisperingly suggested many grievous blasphemies to him which he verily thought had proceeded from his own mind. This put Christian more to it than anything that he met with before, even to think that he should now blaspheme him that he loved so much before; yet, could he have helped it, he would not have done it:

but he had not the discretion neither to stop his ears, nor to know from whence those blasphemies came.

When Christian had travelled in this disconsolate condition some considerable time, he thought he heard the voice of a man, as going before him, saying, '*Though I walk through the Valley of the Shadow of Death, I will fear none ill, for thou art with me.*'

Then he was glad, and that for these reasons:

First, because he gathered from thence, that some who feared God were in this Valley as well as himself.

Secondly, for that he perceived God was with them, though in that dark and dismal state; and why not, thought he, with me, though by reason of the impediment that attends this place I cannot perceive it.

Thirdly, for that he hoped (could he overtake them) to have company by and by. So he went on, and called to him that was before; but he knew not what to answer, for that he also thought himself to be alone: and by and by, the day broke; then said Christian, '*He hath turned the shadow of death into the morning.*'

Now morning being come he looked back, not of desire to return, but to see by the light of the day what hazards he had gone through in the dark. So he saw more perfectly the ditch that was on the one hand, and the quag that was on the other; also how narrow the way was which lay betwixt them both; also now he saw the hobgoblins, and satyrs, and dragons of the pit, but all afar off; for after break of day they came not nigh; yet they were discovered to him, according to that which is written, *He discovereth deep things out of darkness, and bringeth out to light the shadow of death.*

JOHN BUNYAN,
from *The Pilgrim's Progress*

The Tyger

Tyger Tyger, burning bright,
In the forests of the night:
What immortal hand or eye,
Could frame thy fearful symmetry?

In what distant deeps or skies
Burnt the fire of thine eyes!
On what wings dare he aspire?
What the hand, dare sieze the fire?

And what shoulder, & what art,
Could twist the sinews of thy heart?
And when thy heart began to beat,
What dread hand? & what dread feet?

What the hammer? what the chain,
In what furnace was thy brain?
What the anvil? what dread grasp,
Dare its deadly terrors clasp?

When the stars threw down their spears
And water'd heaven with their tears:
Did he smile his work to see?
Did he who made the Lamb make thee?

Tyger, Tyger burning bright,
In the forests of the night:
What immortal hand or eye,
Dare frame thy fearful symmetry?

WILLIAM BLAKE,
from *Songs of Innocence and Experience*

The World (1)

1

I saw Eternity the other night
Like a great *Ring* of pure and endless light,
　　All calm, as it was bright,
And round beneath it, Time in hours, days, years
　　　　Driven by the spheres
Like a vast shadow moved, in which the world
　　　　And all her train were hurled;
The doting lover in his quaintest strain
　　　　Did there complain,
Near him, his lute, his fancy, and his flights,
　　　　Wit's sour delights,
With gloves, and knots the silly snares of pleasure
　　　　Yet his dear treasure
All scattered lay, while he his eyes did pour
　　　　Upon a flower.

2

The darksome states-man hung with weights and woe
Like a thick midnight-fog moved there so slow
　　He did nor stay, nor go;
Condemning thoughts (like sad eclipses) scowl
　　　　Upon his soul,

And clouds of crying witnesses without
 Pursued him with one shout.
Yet digged the mole, and lest his ways be found
  Worked under ground,
Where he did clutch his prey, but one did see
  That policy,
Churches and altars fed him, perjuries
  Were gnats and flies,
It rained about him blood and tears, but he
  Drank them as free.

3

The fearful miser on a heap of rust,
Sat pining all his life there, did scarce trust
 His own hands with the dust,
Yet would not place one piece above, but lives
  In fear of thieves.
Thousands there were as frantic as himself
 And hugged each one his pelf,
The down-right epicure placed heaven in sense
  And scorned pretence
While others slipped into a wide excess
  Said little less;
The weaker sort slight, trivial wares enslave
  Who think them brave,
And poor, despised truth sat counting by
  Their victory.

4

Yet some, who all this while did weep and sing,
And sing, and weep, soared up into the *Ring*,
 But most would use no wing.
O fools (said I,) thus to prefer dark night
  Before true light,

To live in grots, and caves, and hate the day
    Because it shows the way,
The way which from this dead and dark abode
    Leads up to God,
A way where you might tread the Sun, and be
    More bright than he.
But as I did their madness so discuss
    One whispered thus,
This ring the bride-groom did for none provide
    But for his bride.

HENRY VAUGHAN

Dover Beach

The sea is calm to-night.
The tide is full, the moon lies fair
Upon the straits; – on the French coast the light
Gleams and is gone; the cliffs of England stand,
Glimmering and vast, out in the tranquil bay.
Come to the window, sweet is the night-air!
Only, from the long line of spray
Where the sea meets the moon-blanch'd land,
Listen! you hear the grating roar
Of pebbles which the waves draw back, and fling,
At their return, up the high strand,
Begin, and cease, and then again begin,
With tremulous cadence slow, and bring
The eternal note of sadness in.

Sophocles long ago
Heard it on the Aegaean, and it brought
Into his mind the turbid ebb and flow
Of human misery; we
Find also in the sound a thought,
Hearing it by this distant northern sea.

The Sea of Faith
Was once, too, at the full, and round earth's shore
Lay like the folds of a bright girdle furl'd.
But now I only hear
Its melancholy, long, withdrawing roar,
Retreating, to the breath
Of the night-wind, down the vast edges drear
And naked shingles of the world.

Ah, love, let us be true
To one another! for the world, which seems
To lie before us like a land of dreams,
So various, so beautiful, so new,
Hath really neither joy, nor love, nor light,
Nor certitude, nor peace, nor help for pain;
And we are here as on a darkling plain
Swept with confused alarms of struggle and flight,
Where ignorant armies clash by night.

MATTHEW ARNOLD

Witches, and Other Night-Fears

We are too hasty when we set down our ancestors in the gross for fools, for the monstrous inconsistencies (as they seem to us) involved in their creed of witchcraft. In the relations of this visible world we find them to have been as rational, and shrewd to detect an historic anomaly, as ourselves. But when once the invisible world was supposed to be opened, and the lawless agency of bad spirits assumed, what measures of probability, of decency, of fitness, or proportion – of that which distinguishes the likely from the palpable absurd – could they have to guide them in the rejection or admission of any particular testimony? – that maidens pined away, wasting inwardly as their waxen images consumed before a fire – that corn was lodged, and cattle lamed – that whirlwinds uptore in diabolic revelry the oaks of the forests – or that spits and kettles only danced a fearful-innocent vagary about some rustic's kitchen when no wind was stirring – were all equally probable where no law of agency was understood. That the prince of the powers of darkness, passing by the flower and pomp of the earth, should lay preposterous siege to the weak fantasy of indigent eld – has neither likelihood nor unlikelihood *a priori* to us, who have no measure to guess at his policy, or standard to estimate what rate those anile souls may fetch in the devil's market. Nor, when the wicked are expressly symbolized by a goat, was it to be wondered at so much, that *he* should come sometimes in that body, and assert his metaphor. – That the intercourse was opened at all between both worlds was perhaps the mistake – but that once assumed, I see no reason for disbelieving one attested story of this nature more than another on the score of absurdity. There is no law to judge of the lawless, or canon by which a dream may be criticized.

I have sometimes thought that I could not have existed in

the days of received witchcraft; that I could not have slept in a village where one of those reputed hags dwelt. Our ancestors were bolder or more obtuse. Amidst the universal belief that these wretches were in league with the author of all evil, holding hell tributary to their muttering, no simple Justice of the Peace seems to have scrupled issuing, or silly Headborough serving, a warrant upon them – as if they should subpœna Satan! – Prospero in his boat, with his books and wand about him, suffers himself to be conveyed away at the mercy of his enemies to an unknown island. He might have raised a storm or two, we think, on the passage. His acquiescence is in exact analogy to the non-resistance of witches to the constituted powers. – What stops the Fiend in Spenser from tearing Guyon to pieces – or who had made it a condition of his prey, that Guyon must take assay of the glorious bait – we have no guess. We do not know the laws of that country.

From my childhood I was extremely inquisitive about witches and witch-stories. My maid, and more legendary aunt, supplied me with good store. But I shall mention the accident which directed my curiosity originally into this channel. In my father's book-closet, the History of the Bible, by Stackhouse, occupied a distinguished station. The pictures with which it abounds – one of the ark, in particular, and another of Solomon's temple, delineated with all the fidelity of ocular admeasurement, as if the artist had been upon the spot – attracted my childish attention. There was a picture, too, of the Witch raising up Samuel, which I wish that I had never seen. We shall come to that hereafter. Stackhouse is in two huge tomes – and there was a pleasure in removing folios of that magnitude, which, with infinite straining, was as much as I could manage, from the situation which they occupied upon an upper shelf. I have not met with the work from that time to this, but I remember it consisted of Old Testament stories, orderly set down, with the *objection* appended to each story, and the *solution* of the objection regularly tacked to that. The *objection* was a summary of whatever difficulties had been opposed to the credibility of the history, by the shrewdness of ancient or modern infidelity, drawn up with an almost complimentary excess of candour. The *solution* was brief, modest, and satisfactory. The bane and antidote were both before you. To doubts so put, and so squashed, there seemed to be an end for ever. The dragon lay dead, for the foot of the veriest babe to trample on. But – like as was rather feared than realized from that slain monster in Spenser – from the womb of those crushed errors young dragonets would creep, exceeding the prowess of so tender a Saint George as myself to vanquish. The habit of expecting objections to every passage, set me upon starting more objections, for the glory of finding a solution of my own for them. I became staggered and per-plexed, a sceptic in long coats. The pretty Bible stories which I had read, or heard read in church, lost their purity and sincerity of impression, and were turned into so many historic or chrono-logic theses to be defended against whatever impugners. I was not to disbelieve them, but – the next thing to that – I was to be quite sure that some one or other would or had disbelieved them. Next to making a child an infidel, is the letting him know that there are infidels at all. Credulity is the man's weakness, but the child's strength. Oh, how ugly sound scriptural doubts from the mouth of a babe and a suckling! – I should have lost myself in these mazes, and have pined away, I think, with such unfit sustenance as these husks afforded, but for a fortunate piece of ill-fortune, which about this time befel me. Turning over the picture of the ark with too much haste, I unhappily made a breach in its ingenious fabric – driving my inconsiderate fingers right through the two larger quadrupeds – the elephant, and the camel – that stare (as well they might) out of the two last windows next the steerage in that unique piece of naval architecture. Stackhouse was henceforth locked up, and became an interdicted treasure. With the book, the *objections* and *solutions* gradually cleared out of my head, and have seldom returned since in any force to trouble me. – But there was one impression which I had imbibed from Stackhouse, which no lock or bar could shut out, and which was destined to try my childish nerves rather more seriously. – That detestable picture!

I was dreadfully alive to nervous terrors. The night-time solitude, and the dark, were my hell. The sufferings I endured in this nature would justify the expression. I never laid my head on my pillow, I suppose, from the fourth to the seventh or eighth year of my life – so far as memory serves in things so long ago – without an assurance, which realized its own prophecy, of seeing some frightful spectre. Be old Stackhouse then acquitted in part, if I say, that to his picture of the Witch raising up Samuel – (O that old man covered with a mantle!) I owe – not my midnight terrors, the hell of my infancy – but the shape and manner of their visitation. It was he who dressed up for me a hag that nightly sate upon my pillow – a sure bedfellow, when my aunt or my maid was far from me. All day long, while the book was permitted me, I dreamed waking over his delineation, and at night (if I may use so bold an expression) awoke into sleep, and found the vision true. I durst not, even in the daylight, once enter the chamber where I slept, without my face turned to the window, aversely from the bed where my witchridden pillow was. – Parents do not know what they do when they leave tender babes alone to go to sleep in the dark. The feeling about for a friendly arm – the hoping for a familiar voice – when they wake screaming – and find none to soothe them – what a terrible shaking it is to their poor nerves! The keeping them up till midnight, through candle-light and the unwholesome hours, as they are called, – would, I am satisfied, in a medical point of view, prove the better caution. – That detestable picture, as I have said, gave the fashion to my dreams – if dreams they were – for the scene of them was invariably the room in which I lay. Had I never met with the picture, the fears would have come self-pictured in some shape or other –

Headless bear, black man, or ape –

but, as it was, my imaginations took that form. – It is not book, or picture, or the stories of foolish servants, which create these terrors in children. They can at most but give them a direction. Dear little T. H. who of all children has been brought up with the most scrupulous exclusion of every taint of superstition – who was never allowed to hear of goblin or apparition, or scarcely to be told of bad men, or to read or hear of any distressing story – finds all this world of fear, from which he has been so rigidly excluded *ab extra*, in his own 'thick-coming fancies'; and from his little midnight pillow, this nurse-child of optimism will start at shapes, unborrowed of tradition, in sweats to which the reveries of the cell-damned murderer are tranquillity.

Gorgons, and Hydras, and Chimæras dire – stories of Celæno and the Harpies – may reproduce themselves in the brain of superstition – but they were there before. They are transcripts, types – the archetypes are in us, and eternal. How else should the recital of that, which we know in a waking sense to be false, come to affect us at all? – or

– Names, whose sense we see not,
Fray us with things that be not?

Is it that we naturally conceive terror from such objects, considered in their capacity of being able to inflict upon us bodily injury? – O, least of all! These terrors are of older standing. They date beyond body – or, without the body, they would have been the same. All the cruel, tormenting, defined devils in Dante – tearing, mangling, choking, stifling, scorching demons – are they one half so fearful to the spirit of a man, as the simple idea of a spirit unembodied following him –

> Like one that on a lonesome road
> Doth walk in fear and dread,
> And having once turn'd round, walks on,
> And turns no more his head;
> Because he knows a frightful fiend
> Doth close behind him tread.*

That the kind of fear here treated of is purely spiritual – that it is strong in proportion as it is objectless upon earth – that it predominates in the period of sinless infancy – are difficulties, the solution of which might afford some probable insight into our ante-mundane condition, and a peep at least into the shadow-land of pre-existence.

My night-fancies have long ceased to be afflictive. I confess an occasional night-mare; but I do not, as in early youth, keep a stud of them. Fiendish faces, with the extinguished taper, will come and look at me; but I know them for mockeries, even while I cannot elude their presence, and I fight and grapple with them. For the credit of my imagination, I am almost ashamed to say how tame and prosaic my dreams are grown. They are never romantic, seldom even rural. They are of architecture and of buildings – cities abroad, which I have never seen, and hardly have hope to see. I have traversed, for the seeming length of a natural day, Rome, Amsterdam, Paris, Lisbon – their churches, palaces, squares, market-places, shops, suburbs, ruins, with an inexpressible sense of delight – a map-like distinctness of trace – and a daylight vividness of vision, that was all but being awake. – I have formerly travelled among the Westmoreland fells – my highest Alps, – but they are objects too mighty for the grasp of my dreaming recognition; and I have again and again awoke with ineffectual struggles of the inner eye, to make out a shape, in any way whatever, of Helvellyn. Methought I was in that

* Mr Coleridge's Ancient Mariner.

country, but the mountains were gone. The poverty of my dreams mortifies me. There is Coleridge, at his will can conjure up icy domes, and pleasure-houses for Kubla Khan, and Abyssinian maids, and songs of Abara, and caverns,

Where Alph, the sacred river, runs,

to solace his night solitudes – when I cannot muster a fiddle. Barry Cornwall has his tritons and his nereids gamboling before him in nocturnal visions, and proclaiming sons born to Neptune – when my stretch of imaginative activity can hardly, in the night season, raise up the ghost of a fish-wife. To set my failures in somewhat a mortifying light – it was after reading the noble Dream of this poet, that my fancy ran strong upon these marine spectra; and the poor plastic power, such as it is, within me set to work, to humour my folly in a sort of dream that very night. Methought I was upon the ocean billows at some sea nuptials, riding and mounted high, with the customary train sounding their conchs before me, (I myself, you may be sure, the *leading god*,) and jollily we went careering over the main, till just where Ino Leucothea should have greeted me (I think it was Ino) with a white embrace, the billows gradually subsiding, fell from a sea-roughness to a sea-calm, and thence to a river-motion, and that river (as happens in the familiarization of dreams) was no other than the gentle Thames, which landed me, in the wafture of a placid wave or two, alone, safe and inglorious, somewhere at the foot of Lambeth Palace.

The degree of the soul's creativeness in sleep might furnish no whimsical criterion of the quantum of poetical faculty resident in the same soul waking. An old gentleman, a friend of mine, and a humorist, used to carry this notion so far, that when he saw any stripling of his acquaintance ambitious of becoming a poet, his first question would be, – 'Young man, what sort of dreams have you?' I have so much faith in my old friend's theory, that

when I feel that idle vein returning upon me, I presently subside
into my proper element of prose, remembering those eluding
nereids, and that inauspicious inland landing.

CHARLES LAMB

'Death be not proud'

Death be not proud, though some have called thee
Mighty and dreadful, for, thou art not so,
For, those, whom thou think'st, thou dost overthrow,
Die not, poor death, nor yet canst thou kill me;
From rest and sleep, which but thy pictures be,
Much pleasure, then from thee, much more must flow,
And soonest our best men with thee do go,
Rest of their bones, and soul's delivery.
Thou art slave to fate, chance, kings, and desperate men,
And dost with poison, war, and sickness dwell,
And poppy, or charms can make us sleep as well,
And better than thy stroke; why swell'st thou then?
One short sleep past, we wake eternally,
And death shall be no more, Death thou shalt die.

JOHN DONNE

'Care-charmer Sleep,
son of the sable Night'

Care-charmer Sleep, son of the sable Night,
Brother to Death, in silent darkness born,
Relieve my languish, and restore the light;
With dark forgetting of my care return.

And let the day be time enough to mourn
The shipwreck of my ill-adventured youth:
Let waking eyes suffice to wail their scorn,
Without the torment of the night's untruth.

Cease, dreams, the images of day-desires,
To model forth the passions of the morrow;
Never let rising Sun approve you liars,
To add more grief to aggravate my sorrow:

Still let me sleep, embracing clouds in vain,
And never wake to feel the day's disdain.

SAMUEL DANIEL

To Sleep

A flock of sheep that leisurely pass by
One after one; the sound of rain, and bees
Murmuring; the fall of rivers, winds and seas,
Smooth fields, white sheets of water, and pure sky;
I've thought of all by turns, and yet do lie
Sleepless; and soon the small birds' melodies
Must hear, first utter'd from my orchard trees,
And the first cuckoo's melancholy cry.
Even thus last night, and two nights more I lay,
And could not win thee, Sleep! by any stealth:
So do not let me wear to-night away:
Without Thee what is all the morning's wealth?
Come, blessèd barrier between day and day,
Dear mother of fresh thoughts and joyous health!

WILLIAM WORDSWORTH

Corruption

Sure, it was so. Man in those early days
  Was not all stone, and earth,
He shined a little, and by those weak rays
  Had some glimpse of his birth.
He saw Heaven o'er his head, and knew from whence
  He came (condemned,) hither,
And, as first love draws strongest, so from hence
  His mind sure progressed thither.
Things here were strange unto him: sweat, and till
  All was a thorn, or weed,
Nor did those last, but (like himself,) died still
  As soon as they did *seed*,
They seemed to quarrel with him; for that act
  That fell him, foiled them all,
He drew the curse upon the world, and cracked
  The whole frame with his fall.
This made him long for *home*, as loath to stay
  With murmurers, and foes;
He sighed for *Eden*; and would often say
  Ah! what bright days were those?
Nor was Heaven cold unto him; for each day
  The valley, or the mountain
Afforded visits, and still *Paradise* lay
  In some green shade, or fountain.
Angels lay *leiger* here; each bush, and cell,
  Each oak, and high-way knew them,
Walk but the fields, or sit down at some *well*,
  And he was sure to view them.
Almighty *Love*! where art thou now? mad man
  Sits down, and freezeth on,

He raves, and swears to stir nor fire, nor fan,
    But bids the thread be spun.
I see, thy curtains are close-drawn; thy bow
    Looks dim too in the cloud,
Sin triumphs still, and man is sunk below
    The centre, and his shroud;
All's in deep sleep, and night; thick darkness lies
    And hatcheth o'er thy people;
But hark! what trumpet's that? what Angel cries
    Arise! Thrust in thy sickle.

HENRY VAUGHAN

from *Urne-Buriall*

In a Field of old *Walsingham*, not many moneths past, were digged up between fourty and fifty Urnes, deposited in a dry and sandy soile, not a yard deep, nor farre from one another: Not all strictly of one figure, but most answering these described: Some containing two pounds of bones, distinguishable in skulls, ribs, jawes, thigh-bones, and teeth, with fresh impressions of their combustion. Besides the extraneous substances like peeces of small boxes, or combes handsomely wrought, handles of small brasse instruments, brazen nippers, and in one some kinde of *Opale.*

Near the same plot of ground, for about six yards compasse were digged up coals and incinerated substances, which begat conjecture that this was the *Ustrina* or place of burning their bodies or some sacrificing place unto the *Manes*, which was properly below the surface of the ground, as the *Aræ* and Altars unto the gods and *Heroes* above it.

That these were the Urnes of *Romanes* from the common custome and place where they were found, is no obscure conjecture, not farre from a *Romane* Garrison, and but five Miles from *Brancaster*, set down by ancient Record under the name of *Brannodunum*. And where the adjoyning Towne, containing seven Parishes, in no very different sound, but Saxon Termination, still retains the Name of *Burnham*, which being an early station, it is not improbable the neighbour parts were filled with habitations, either of *Romanes* themselves, or *Brittains Romanised*, which observed the *Romane* customes.

* * *

Now since these dead bones have already out-lasted the living ones of *Methuselah*, and in a yard under ground, and thin walls of clay, out-worn all the strong and specious buildings above it; and quietly rested under the drums and tramplings of three conquests; What Prince can promise such diuturnity unto his Reliques, or might not gladly say,

Sic ego componi versus in ossa velim.*

Time which antiquates Antiquities, and hath an art to make dust of all things, hath yet spared these *minor* Monuments. In vain we hope to be known by open and visible conservatories, when to be unknown was the means of their continuation and obscurity their protection: If they dyed by violent hands, and were thrust into their Urnes, these bones become considerable, and some old Philosophers would honour them, whose souls they conceived most pure, which were thus snatched from their bodies; and to retain a stranger propension unto them: whereas they weariedly left a languishing corps, and with faint desires of re-union. If they fell by long and aged decay, yet wrapt up in the bundle of time, they fall into indistinction, and make but one blot with Infants. If we begin to die when we live, and long

---

* Thus, when naught is left of me but bones, would I be laid to rest.

life be but a prolongation of death; our life is a sad composition; We live with death, and die not in a moment. How many pulses made up the life of *Methuselah*, were work for *Archimedes*: Common Counters summe up the life of *Moses* his man. Our dayes become considerable like pretty sums by minute accumulations; where numerous fractions make up but small round numbers; and our dayes of a span long make not one little finger.

If the nearnesse of our last necessity, brought a nearer con-formity unto it, there were a happinesse in hoary hairs, and no calamity in half senses. But the long habit of living indisposeth us for dying; When Avarice makes us the sport of death; When even *David* grew politickly cruell; and *Solomon* could hardly be said to be the wisest of men. But many are too early old, and before the date of age. Adversity stretcheth our dayes, misery makes *Alcmenas* nights, and time hath no wings unto it. But the most tedious being is that which can unwish it self, content to be nothing, or never to have been, which was beyond the *male*-content of *Job*, who cursed not the day of his life, but his Nativity: Content to have so farre been, as to have a Title to future being; Although he had lived here but in an hidden state of life, and as it were an abortion.

What Song the *Syrens* sang, or what name *Achilles* assumed when he hid himself among women, though puzling Questions are not beyond all conjecture. What time the persons of these Ossuaries entred the famous Nations of the dead, and slept with Princes and Counsellours, might admit a wide solution. But who were the proprietaries of these bones, or what bodies these ashes made up, were a question above Antiquarism. Not to be resolved by man, nor easily perhaps by spirits, except we consult the Provinciall Guardians, or tutelary Observators. Had they made as good provision for their names, as they have done for their Reliques, they had not so grosly erred in the art of perpetuation. But to subsist in bones, and be put Pyramidally extant, is a fallacy in duration. Vain ashes, which in the oblivion of names, persons, times, and sexes, have found unto themselves, a fruitlesse continuation, and only arise unto late posterity, as Emblemes of mortall vanities; Antidotes against pride, vain-glory, and madding vices. Pagan vain-glories which thought the world might last for ever, had encouragement for ambition, and finding no *Atropos* unto the immortality of their Names, were never dampt with the necessity of oblivion. Even old ambitions had the advantage of ours, in the attempts of their vain-glories, who acting early, and before the probable Meridian of time, have by this time found great accomplishment of their designes, whereby the ancient *Heroes* have already out-lasted their Monuments, and Mechanicall preservations. But in this latter Scene of time we cannot expect such Mummies unto our memories, when ambition may fear the Prophecy of *Elias*, and *Charles* the fifth can never hope to live within two *Methusela's* of *Hector*.

And therefore restlesse inquietude for the diuturnity of our memories unto present considerations, seems a vanity almost out of date, and superanuated peece of folly. We cannot hope to live so long in our names, as some have done in their persons, one face of *Janus* holds no proportion unto the other. 'Tis too late to be ambitious. The great mutations of the world are acted, or time may be too short for our designes. To extend our memories by Monuments, whose death we dayly pray for, and whose duration we cannot hope, without injury to our expectations, in the advent of the last day, were a contradiction to our beliefs. We whose generations are ordained in this setting part of time, are providentially taken off from such imaginations. And being necessitated to eye the remaining particle of futurity, are naturally constituted unto thoughts of the next world, and cannot excusably decline the consideration of that duration, which maketh Pyramids pillars of snow, and all that's past a moment.

Circles and right lines limit and close all bodies, and the mortall right-lined circle, must conclude and shut up all. There is no antidote against the *Opium* of time, which temporally considereth all things; Our Fathers finde their graves in our short memories, and sadly tell us how we may be buried in our Survivors. Grave-stones tell truth scarce fourty years. Generations passe while some trees stand, and old Families last not three Oaks. To be read by bare Inscriptions like many in *Gruter*, to hope for Eternity by Ænigmaticall Epithetes, or first letters of our names, to be studied by Antiquaries, who we were, and have new Names given us like many of the Mummies, are cold consolations unto the Students of perpetuity, even by everlasting Languages.

To be content that times to come should only know there was such a man, not caring whether they knew more of him, was a frigid ambition in *Cardan*; disparaging his horoscopal inclination and judgement of himself, who cares to subsist like *Hippocrates* Patients, or *Achilles* horses in *Homer*, under naked nominations, without deserts and noble acts, which are the balsame of our memories, the *Entelechia* and soul of our subsistences. To be namelesse in worthy deeds exceeds an infamous history. The *Canaanitish* woman lives more happily without a name, then *Herodias* with one. And who had not rather have been the good theef, then *Pilate*?

But the iniquity of oblivion blindely scattereth her poppy, and deals with the memory of men without distinction to merit of perpetuity. Who can but pity the founder of the Pyramids? *Herostratus* lives that burnt the Temple of *Diana*, he is almost lost that built it; Time hath spared the Epitaph of *Adrians* horse, confounded that of himself. In vain we compute our felicities by the advantage of our good names, since bad have equall durations; and *Thersites* is like to live as long as *Agamemnon*. Who knows whether the best of men be known? or whether there be not more remarkable persons forgot, then any that stand remembered in the known account of time? without the favour of the everlasting Register the first man had been as unknown as the last, and *Methuselahs* long life had been his only Chronicle.

Oblivion is not to be hired: The greater part must be content to be as though they had not been, to be found in the Register of God, not in the record of man. Twenty seven Names make up the first story, and the recorded names ever since contain not one living Century. The number of the dead long exceedeth all that shall live. The night of time far surpasseth the day, and who knows when was the Æquinox? Every houre addes unto that current Arithmetique, which scarce stands one moment. And since death must be the *Lucina* of life, and even Pagans could doubt whether thus to live, were to dye. Since our longest Sunne sets at right descensions, and makes but winter arches, and therefore it cannot be long before we lie down in darknesse, and have our light in ashes. Since the brother of death daily haunts us with dying *memento*'s, and time that grows old it self, bids us hope no long duration: Diuturnity is a dream and folly of expectation.

Darknesse and light divide the course of time, and oblivion snares with memory, a great part even of our living beings; we slightly remember our felicities, and the smartest stroaks of affliction leave but short smart upon us. Sense endureth no extremities, and sorrows destroy us or themselves. To weep into stones are fables. Afflictions induce callosities, miseries are slippery, or fall like snow upon us, which notwithstanding is no unhappy stupidity. To be ignorant of evils to come, and forgetfull of evils past, is a mercifull provision in nature, whereby we digest the mixture of our few and evil dayes, and our delivered senses not relapsing into cutting remembrances, our sorrows are not kept raw by the edge of repetitions. A great part of Antiquity contented their hopes of subsistency with a transmigration of their souls. A good way to continue their memories, while having the advantage of plurall successions, they could not but act something remarkable in such variety of beings, and enjoying the fame of their passed selves, make accumulation of glory unto their last durations. Others rather than be lost in the uncomfortable night of nothing, were content to recede into the common being, and make one particle of the publick soul of all things, which was no more then to return into their unknown and divine Originall again. Ægyptian ingenuity was more unsatisfied, contriving their bodies in sweet consistences, to attend the return of their souls. But all was vanity, feeding the winde, and folly. The Ægyptian Mummies, which *Cambyses* or time hath spared, avarice now consumeth. Mummie is become Merchandise, *Mizraim* cures wounds, and *Pharaoh* is sold for balsoms.

In vain do individuals hope for Immortality, or any patent from oblivion, in preservations below the Moon: Men have been deceived even in their flatteries about the Sun, and studied conceits to perpetuate their names in heaven. The various Cosmography of that part hath already varied the names of contrived constellations; *Nimrod* is lost in *Orion*, and *Osyris* in the Doggestarre. While we look for incorruption in the heavens, we finde they are but like the Earth; Durable in their main bodies, alterable in their parts: whereof beside Comets and new Stars, perspectives begin to tell tales. And the spots that wander about the Sun, with *Phaetons* favour, would make clear conviction.

There is nothing strictly immortall, but immortality; whatever hath no beginning may be confident of no end. All others have a dependent being, and within the reach of destruction, which is the peculiar of that necessary essence that cannot destroy it self; And the highest strain of omnipotency to be so powerfully constituted, as not to suffer even from the power of it self. But the sufficiency of Christian Immortality frustrates all earthly glory, and the quality of either state after death, makes a folly of posthumous memory. God who can only destroy our souls, and hath assured our resurrection, either of our bodies or names hath directly promised no duration. Wherein there is so much of a chance that the boldest Expectants have found unhappy frustration; and to hold long subsistence, seems but a scape in oblivion. But man is a Noble Animal, splendid in ashes, and pompous in the grave, solemnizing Nativities and Deaths with equall lustre, nor omitting Ceremonies of bravery, in the infamy of his nature.

Life is a pure flame, and we live by an invisible Sun within us. A small fire sufficeth for life, great flames seemed too little after death, while men vainly affected precious pyres, and to burn like *Sardanapalus*, but the wisedom of funerall Laws found the folly of prodigall blazes, and reduced undoing fires, unto the rule of sober obsequies, wherein few could be so mean as not to provide wood, pitch, a mourner, and an Urne.

Five Languages secured not the Epitaph of *Gordianus*; The man of God lives longer without a Tomb then any by one, invisibly interred by Angels, and adjudged to obscurity, though not without some marks directing humane discovery. *Enoch* and *Elias* without either tomb or buriall, in an anomalous state of being, are the great Examples of perpetuity, in their long and living memory, in strict account being still on this side death, and having a late part yet to act upon this stage of earth. If in the decretory term of the world we shall not all dye but be changed, according to received translation; the last day will make but few graves; at least quick Resurrections will anticipate lasting Sepultures; Some Graves will be opened before they be quite closed, and *Lazarus* be no wonder. When many that feared to dye shall groane that they can dye but once, the dismall state is the second and living death, when life puts despair on the damned; when men shall wish the coverings of Mountaines, not of Monuments, and annihilation shall be courted.

While some have studied Monuments, others have studiously declined them: and some have been so vainly boisterous, that they durst not acknowledge their Graves; wherein *Alaricus* seems most subtle, who had a River turned to hide his bones at the bottome. Even *Sylla* that thought himself safe in his Urne, could not prevent revenging tongues, and stones thrown at his Monument. Happy are they whom privacy makes innocent, who deal so with men in this world, that they are not afraid to meet them in the next, who when they dye, make no commotion among the dead, and are not toucht with that poeticall taunt of *Isaiah.*

Pyramids, Arches, Obelisks, were but the irregularities of vainglory, and wilde enormities of ancient magnanimity. But the most magnanimous resolutions rests in the Christian Religion, which trampleth upon pride, and sets on the neck of ambition, humbly pursuing that infallible perpetuity, unto which all others must diminish their diameters, and be poorly seen in Angles of contingency.

Pious spirits who passed their dayes in raptures of futurity, made little more of this world, then the world that was before it, while they lay obscure in the Chaos of pre-ordination, and night of their fore-beings. And if any have been so happy as truly to understand Christian annihilation, extasis, exolution, liquefaction, transformation, the kisse of the Spouse, gustation of God, and ingression into the divine shadow, they have already had an handsome anticipation of heaven; the glory of the world is surely over, and the earth in ashes unto them.

To subsist in lasting Monuments, to live in their productions, to exist in their names, and prædicament of *Chymera*'s, was large satisfaction unto old expectations, and made one part of their *Elyziums.* But all this is nothing in the Metaphysicks of true belief. To live indeed is to be again our selves, which being not only an hope but an evidence in noble beleevers; 'Tis all one to lye in St *Innocents* Church-yard, as in the Sands of Ægypt: Ready to be any thing, in the extasie of being ever, and as content with six foot as the Moles of *Adrianus.*

SIR THOMAS BROWNE

Channel Firing

That night your great guns, unawares,
Shook all our coffins as we lay,
And broke the chancel window-squares,
We thought it was the Judgment-day

And sat upright. While drearisome
Arose the howl of wakened hounds:
The mouse let fall the altar-crumb,
The worms drew back into the mounds,

The glebe cow drooled. Till God called, 'No;
It's gunnery practice out at sea
Just as before you went below;
The world is as it used to be:

'All nations striving strong to make
Red war yet redder. Mad as hatters
They do no more for Christés sake
Than you who are helpless in such matters.

'That this is not the judgment-hour
For some of them's a blessed thing,
For if it were they'd have to scour
Hell's floor for so much threatening . . .

'Ha, ha. It will be warmer when
I blow the trumpet (if indeed
I ever do; for you are men,
And rest eternal sorely need).'

So down we lay again. 'I wonder,
Will the world ever saner be,'
Said one, 'than when He sent us under
In our indifferent century!'

And many a skeleton shook his head.
'Instead of preaching forty year,'
My neighbour Parson Thirdly said,
'I wish I had stuck to pipes and beer.'

Again the guns disturbed the hour,
Roaring their readiness to avenge,
As far inland as Stourton Tower,
And Camelot, and starlit Stonehenge.

THOMAS HARDY

Author Notes

All publication dates given refer to the original publication of the Penguin edition.

JOSEPH ADDISON (1672–1719). 'Ghosts' from *Selections from the Tatler and the Spectator* (1982, 0 14 043298 1) and 'The Tombs in Westminster Abbey' from *A Book of English Essays* (1951, 0 14 043153 5).

JOHN ARBUTHNOT (1667–1735). 'Know Yourself' from *Eighteenth-Century English Verse* (1973, 0 14 042169 6).

MATTHEW ARNOLD (1822–88). Both poems from *Selected Poems* (1994, 0 14 042376 1).

WILLIAM BARNES (1801–86). 'Evenèn in the Village' from *Selected Poems* (1994, 0 14 042379 6).

FRANCIS BEAUMONT (1584–1616). 'On the Tombs in Westminster Abbey' from Frances Turner Palgrave's *The Golden Treasury* (1991, 0 14 042364 8).

WILLIAM BLAKE (1757–1837). All poems from *The Complete Poems* (1977, 0 14 042215 3) with punctuation added to 'A Memorable Fancy'.

EMILY BRONTË (1818–48). 'The Night is darkening around me' from *The Penguin Book of Victorian Verse* (Allen Lane, 1997, 07139 9049 X).

SIR THOMAS BROWNE (1605–82). All extracts from *The Major Works* (1977, 0 14 043109 8).

JOHN BUNYAN (1628–88). 'The Valley of the Shadow of Death' from *The Pilgrim's Progress* (1965, 0 14 043004 0).

ROBERT BURNS (1759–96). Both poems from *Selected Poems* (1993, 0 14 042382 6).

GEORGE GORDON, LORD BYRON (1788–1824). 'So We'll Go No More a Roving' from *Selected Poems* (1996, 0 14 04 2381 8) and 'Lines Inscribed upon a Cup Formed from a Skull' from *The Penguin Book of English Romantic Verse* (1968, 0 14 042102 5).

THOMAS CAMPION (1567–1620). 'Now winter nights enlarge' from *The Penguin Book of Renaissance Verse* (1992, 0 14 042346 x).

JOHN CLARE (1793–1864). Psalm 102 from *The Psalms in English* (1996, 0 14 044618 4).

MARY ELIZABETH COLERIDGE (1861–1907). 'Night is fallen within, without' from *The Penguin Book of Victorian Verse* (Allen Lane, 1997, 07139 9049 x).

SAMUEL TAYLOR COLERIDGE (1772–1834). All three poems from *The Complete Poems* (1997, 0 14 042353 2).

MILES COVERDALE (1488–1568). Psalm 102 from *The Psalms in English* (1996, 0 14 044618 4).

WILLIAM COWPER (1731–1800). 'Walking with God' from *Eighteenth-Century English Verse* (1973, 0 14 042169 6).

SAMUEL DANIEL (1563–1619). 'Care charmer Sleep, son of the sable Night' from Francis Turner Palgrave's *The Golden Treasury* (1991, 0 14 042364 8).

THOMAS DE QUINCEY (1785–1859). 'The Terrors of Opium' from *Confessions of an English Opium Eater* (1971, 0 14 043061 x).

CHARLES DICKENS (1812–70) 'Night Walks' from *Selected Journalism, 1850–1870* (1997, 0 14 043580 8).

JOHN DONNE (1572–1631). All prose extracts from *Selected Prose* (1987, 0 14 043239 6). All poems available in *The Complete English Poems* (1971, 0 14 042209 9). 'A Nocturnall upon S. Lucies day, Being the shortest day' in its original spelling from *The Penguin Book of Renaissance Verse* (1992, 0 14 042346 x).

JOHN HALL (1627–56). 'On an Houre glasse' from *The Metaphysical Poets* (1957, 0 14 042038 x).

THOMAS HARDY (1840–1928). All poems appear in *Selected Poems* (1993, 0 14 043341 4).

WILLIAM HAZLITT (1778–1830). 'Dreaming' from *Selected Writings* (1970, 0 14 043050 4).

EDWARD, LORD HERBERT OF CHERBURY (1583–1648). 'To his Watch, when he could not sleep' from *The Metaphysical Poets* (1957, 0 14 042038 x).

GEORGE HERBERT (1593–1633). 'The Pulley', 'The Glance' and 'Evensong' from *The Complete English Poems* (1991, 0 14 042348 6). 'Mortification' from *The Metaphysical Poets* (1957, 0 14 042038 x). 'The Collar' from *The Penguin Book of Renaissance Verse* (1992, 0 14 042346 x).

GERARD MANLEY HOPKINS (1844–89). 'I wake and feel the fell of dark, not day' from *Poems and Prose* (1953, 0 14 042015 0).

BEN JONSON (1572?–1637). 'Inviting a Friend to Supper' from *The Penguin Book of Renaissance Verse* (1992, 0 14 042346 x).

JOHN KEATS (1795–1831). Both poems from *The Complete Poems* (1973, 0 14 042210 2).

HENRY KING (1592–1669). 'My Midnight Meditation' from *The Metaphysical Poets* (1957, 0 14 042038 x). 'An Exequy To his matchlesse never to be forgotten Freind' from *The Penguin Book of Renaissance Verse* (1992, 0 14 042346 x).

CHARLES LAMB (1775–1834). 'Witches, and other Night Fears' from *Selected Prose* (1985, 0 14 043238 8).

CHRISTOPHER MARLOWE (1564–93). 'Faustus Summons Mephostophilis' from *The Complete Plays* (1969, 0 14 043037 7).

ANDREW MARVELL (1621–78). 'The Mower to the Glo Worms' in this spelling from *The Penguin Book of Renaissance Verse* (1992, 0 14 042346 x). See also Marvell's *The Complete Poems* (1972, 0 14 042213 7).

THOMAS NASHE (1567-c.1600). All extracts from *The Unfortunate Traveller and Other Works* (1972, 0 14 043067 9).

MARGARET CAVENDISH, DUCHESS OF NEWCASTLE (1623–73). 'Of Many Worlds in this World' from *The Penguin Book of Renaissance Verse* (1992, 0 14 042346 x).

JOHN NORRIS OF BEMERTON (1657–1711). 'Hymn to Darkness' from *The Metaphysical Poets* (1957, 0 14 042038 x).

EDGAR ALLAN POE (1809–41). 'The City in the Sea' from *The Penguin Book of English Romantic Verse* (1968, 0 14 042102 5).

ALEXANDER POPE (1688–1744). Extract from the 'Illiad, Book VIII' in Pope's *The Iliad of Homer* (1996, 0 14 044504 8).

SIR WALTER RALEIGH (c.1552–1618). 'Even suche is tyme that takes in trust' from *The Penguin Book of Renaissance Verse* (1992, 0 14 042346 x)

THOMAS RAVENSCROFT (dates unknown). 'A Belman's Song' from *The Penguin Book of Renaissance Verse* (1992, 0 14 042346 x)

WILLIAM SHAKESPEARE (1564–1616). Extracts taken from plays taken from *Henry IV Part One* (1968, 0 14 070718 2), *Macbeth* (1967, 0 14 070705 0) , *Measure for Measure* (1969, 0 14 0707015 8), *A Midsummer Night's Dream* (1967, 0 14 070702 6) , *Richard II* (1969, 0 14 070719 0). The sonnets are all taken from *The Sonnets and A Lover's Complaint* (1986, 0 14 070732 8) and the original-spelling version of the sonnet 'Devouring time blunt thou the Lyons pawes' from *The Penguin Book of Renaissance Verse* (1992, 0 14 042346 x).

PERCY BYSSHE SHELLEY (1792–1822). Both poems from Francis Turner Palgrave's *The Golden Treasury* (1991, 0 14 042364 8)

SIR PHILIP SIDNEY (1554–86). Both poems from *Selected Poems* (1994, 0 14 042378 8).

ROBERT SIDNEY (EARL OF LEICESTER, 1554–86). 'Songe 17' from *The Penguin Book of Renaissance Verse* (1992, 0 14 042346 x).

ROBERT SOUTHWELL (1561?–95). 'The burning Babe' from *The Penguin Book of Renaissance Verse* (1992, 0 14 042346 x).

NAHUM TATE (1652–1715) AND NICHOLAS BRADY. Psalm 102 from *The Psalms in English* (1996, 0 14 044618 4).

ALFRED LORD TENNYSON (1809–1892). 'Over the dark world flies wind' from *Selected Poems* (1991, 0 14 044545 5).

JAMES THOMSON (1834–82). Extract from 'The City of Dreadful Night' in *The Penguin Book of Victorian Verse* (Allen Lane, 1997, 07139 9049 x).

CHIDIOCK TICHBORNE (1558?–86). 'Tichborne's Elegy' from *The Penguin Book of Renaissance Verse* (1992, 0 14 042346 x).

HENRY VAUGHAN (*c.*1621–1695). All poems from *The Complete Poems* (1976, 0 14 042208 0).

ISAAC WATTS (1674–1748). 'Psalm 102' from *The Psalms in English* (1996, 0 14 044618 4).

JOHN WEBSTER (*c.*1580–1638). 'Hark, now everything is still' from *Three Plays* (1972, 0 14 043081 4).

WALT WHITMAN (1819–1892). Both poems from *The Complete Poems* (1975, 0 14 042222 6).

OSCAR WILDE (1854–1900). 'On Waking Early' from *The Picture of Dorian Gray* (1985, 0 14 043187 X).

ANNE FINCH, COUNTESS OF WINCHILSEA (1661–1720). 'A Nocturnal Rëverie' from *Eighteenth-Century English Verse* (1973, 0 14 042169 6).

MARY WOLLSTONECRAFT (1759–97). 'Summer on the Baltic' from *A Short Residence in Sweden* (1987, 0 14 043269 8).

WILLIAM WORDSWORTH (1770–1850). 'It is a beauteous evening, calm and free' from *Selected Poems* (1994, 0 14 042375 3). 'To Sleep' from Francis Turner Palgrave's *The Golden Treasury* (1991, 0 14 042364 8).

SIR THOMAS WYATT (1503–42). 'Th'en'my of life, decayer of all kind' from *The Complete Poems* (1978, 0 14 042227 7) and Psalm 102 from *The Psalms in English* (1996, 0 14 044618 4).

EDWARD YOUNG (1683–1765). The extract from 'The Complaint: or, Night Thoughts on Life, Death and Immortality' in *Eighteenth-Century English Verse* (1973, 0 14 042169 6).

**The Penguin Classics and Twentieth-Century Classics
series now include over 1,000 titles and encompass the very
best writing from around the world, an extraordinary wealth
of literature and non-fiction from ancient civilizations to the
present day.**

With *Night Thoughts*, we are delighted to be able to offer you £1
off the Penguin Black Classic or Penguin Twentieth-Century Classic
of your choice. Please see the voucher below.

TO THE CUSTOMER:

To obtain £1 off, please fill in the details below and hand in the completed
voucher to the cashier when purchasing any Penguin Black Classic or
Penguin Twentieth-Century Classic.

Name _____

Address _____

_____*Postcode* _____

**This voucher is only valid against the purchase of a Penguin Black Classic
or Penguin Twentieth-Century Classic. The offer does not apply to audio books.
This offer ends on 1st July 1998 and is only valid in the UK and Republic of Ireland.**
All information will be treated in confidence and will not be passed on to any other organization.

☐ Tick here if you do not wish to receive any further information from Penguin Books.

TO THE BOOKSHOP - BOOKSHOP USE ONLY

Please accept this voucher as £1 discount against the purchase of any
Penguin Black Classic or Penguin Twentieth-Century Classic, made
no later than 1st July 1998.

Name _____

Address _____

_____*Postcode* _____

Penguin account number _____

Signature _____

This voucher is only redeemable against purchase of a Penguin Black Classic
or Penguin Twentieth-Century Classic, made no later than 1/7/98,
and does not apply to audio books.

To receive credit on your account, please return completed vouchers to:
**Night Thoughts Voucher Offer,
Penguin Press Marketing Department, 27 Wrights Lane, London W8 5TZ.**

Incomplete vouchers or those returned after 1/8/98 will not be valid.

If you have a query on your account please telephone your customer services
coordinator.

READ MORE IN PENGUIN

In every corner of the world, on every subject under the sun, Penguin represents quality and variety – the very best in publishing today.

For complete information about books available from Penguin – including Puffins, Penguin Classics and Arkana – and how to order them, write to us at the appropriate address below. Please note that for copyright reasons the selection of books varies from country to country.

In the United Kingdom: Please write to *Dept. EP, Penguin Books Ltd, Bath Road, Harmondsworth, West Drayton, Middlesex UB7 ODA*

In the United States: Please write to *Consumer Sales, Penguin USA, P.O. Box 999, Dept. 17109, Bergenfield, New Jersey 07621-0120*. VISA and MasterCard holders call 1-800-253-6476 to order Penguin titles

In Canada: Please write to *Penguin Books Canada Ltd, 10 Alcorn Avenue, Suite 300, Toronto, Ontario M4V 3B2*

In Australia: Please write to *Penguin Books Australia Ltd, P.O. Box 257, Ringwood, Victoria 3134*

In New Zealand: Please write to *Penguin Books (NZ) Ltd, Private Bag 102902, North Shore Mail Centre, Auckland 10*

In India: Please write to *Penguin Books India Pvt Ltd, 706 Eros Apartments, 56 Nehru Place, New Delhi 110 019*

In the Netherlands: Please write to *Penguin Books Netherlands bv, Postbus 3507, NL-1001 AH Amsterdam*

In Germany: Please write to *Penguin Books Deutschland GmbH, Metzlerstrasse 26, 60594 Frankfurt am Main*

In Spain: Please write to *Penguin Books S. A., Bravo Murillo 19, 1° B, 28015 Madrid*

In Italy: Please write to *Penguin Italia s.r.l., Via Felice Casati 20, I–20124 Milano*

In France: Please write to *Penguin France S. A., 17 rue Lejeune, F–31000 Toulouse*

In Japan: Please write to *Penguin Books Japan, Ishikiribashi Building, 2-5-4, Suido, Bunkyo-ku, Tokyo 112*

In South Africa: Please write to *Longman Penguin Southern Africa (Pty) Ltd, Private Bag X08, Bertsham 2013*